BILLIE EILISH

BILLIE EILISH

THE UNOFFICIAL BIOGRAPHY

FROM E-GIRL
TO ICON

ADRIAN BESLEY

 ZEST BOOKS
MINNEAPOLIS

First American edition published in 2021 by Zest Books™

Copyright © Michael O'Mara Books Limited 2020
First published in Great Britain in 2020 by Michael O'Mara Books Limited
Published by arrangement with Michael O'Mara Books Limited

Zest Books™
An imprint of Lerner Publishing Group, Inc.
241 First Avenue North
Minneapolis, MN 55401 USA

For reading levels and more information, look up this title at www.lernerbooks.com.
Visit us at zestbooks.net. 🅕 🅔

Front and back cover photography: Luigi Rizzo/Pacific Press via ZUMA Wire/Shutterstock

Main body text set in Trade Gothic LT Std Light.
Typeface provided by Adobe Systems.

Library of Congress Cataloging-in-Publication Data

Names: Besley, Adrian, author.
Title: Billie Eilish, the unofficial biography : from e-girl to icon / Adrian Besley.
Description: Minneapolis : Zest Books, 2021. | Includes bibliographical references and index. | Audience: Ages 13–18 | Audience: Grades 7–9 | Summary: "Billie Eilish is a phenomenon, a teenager whose beautifully crafted hits defy categorization and whose defiant persona mirrors the attitudes of a generation. Explore the life, talent, and philosophy of the fastest-rising star in pop music" —Provided by publisher.
Identifiers: LCCN 2020033415 (print) | LCCN 2020033416 (ebook) |
ISBN 9781728424163 (library binding) | ISBN 9781728424170 (paperback) |
ISBN 9781728424187 (ebook)
Subjects: LCSH: Eilish, Billie, 2001—Juvenile literature. | Singers—United States—Biography—Juvenile literature.
Classification: LCC ML3930.E35 B47 2021 (print) | LCC ML3930.E35 (ebook) |
DDC 782.42164092 [B]—dc23

LC record available at https://lccn.loc.gov/2020033415
LC ebook record available at https://lccn.loc.gov/2020033416

Manufactured in the United States of America
1-49266-49386-10/8/2020

CONTENTS

INTRODUCTION 7

CHAPTER ONE
HOMESCHOOL DAYS 11

CHAPTER TWO
OVERNIGHT SENSATION 23

CHAPTER THREE
THE REAL DEAL 35

CHAPTER FOUR
BELLYACHE 47

CHAPTER FIVE
DONT SMILE 59

CHAPTER SIX
ON THE ROAD 71

CHAPTER SEVEN
THE ONE TO WATCH 85

CHAPTER EIGHT
LOVELY 97

CHAPTER NINE
WEARING THE CROWN 109

CHAPTER TEN
BLOHSH 123

CHAPTER ELEVEN
THE MONSTER
UNDER THE BED 135

CHAPTER TWELVE
FOURTEEN PIECES OF ART 149

CHAPTER THIRTEEN
FESTIVAL GIRL 161

CHAPTER FOURTEEN
FINNEAS 173

CHAPTER FIFTEEN
HAPPY NOW... 185

CHAPTER SIXTEEN
GRAMMYS, OSCARS,
AND JAMES BOND 199

ACKNOWLEDGMENTS 213

PICTURE CREDITS 215

INDEX 217

INTRODUCTION

"She's so young!" People have been saying that about Billie Eilish since 2013.

Long before her incredible start to 2020, when she swept the board at the GRAMMYs and had a hit single with the James Bond theme "No Time to Die." When she had a viral hit on SoundCloud, they marveled at her age. When she rocked Coachella, she was a teen sensation. And when she had a US Number 1 in 2019, she was heralded as the first artist born in the twenty-first century to top the *Billboard* 200.

And yet Billie has never defined herself by her age. She's never tried to hide it or play on it. She's worn her Gen Z heart on her sleeve, because that's who she is—but she's a whole lot more besides that. Billie is a wonderfully creative person, as interested in filmmaking, dance, fashion, and art as she is in music. She won't be restrained by music or fashion genres. She's a natural performer who can communicate as well with a twenty-thousand-strong festival crowd as she can with an intimate club audience. She's family-centered and close to her brother, mother, and father. She's a sensitive soul who has suffered with bouts of depression, and she has an intelligent, engaging, and very funny personality.

Billie has always been an open book. For a long time, she bared her heart and soul on social media, and she still gives full and frank answers to even the most difficult questions. In the *Vanity Fair* interviews, which have taken place every year, she is sometimes aghast at or amused by the responses of her younger self, but she is never embarrassed. That was who she was then, and this is who she is now—people change.

However, there is one thing that remains constant. Billie has always known what she wants. You hear it from her brother and musical collaborator, Finneas, from her parents, from her managers, and from Billie herself. Why would she want to create something just because somebody else wants her to do it? Her success has been driven as much by her creative vision and her single-minded desire to make it come to life as it has by her singing and songwriting talent or her ability to perform.

This is the story of a girl who has, by being true to herself, found that millions relate to her, and who has, by making songs she likes, created music that is loved all around the world. It may only be the beginning of what will turn out to be a long journey, but what a journey it has already been . . .

CHAPTER ONE
HOMESCHOOL DAYS

Billie Eilish's first song was about falling into a black hole.

She was just four when she wrote it, and although she was astonishingly young when she became a star, at that age even she was still a work in progress. However, the fact that she wrote it, and continued to write songs through her childhood (on James Corden's "Carpool Karaoke" she shared "What a Wonderful Life," a song she wrote with a friend when she was seven), gives some insight into the creativity and desire to perform she had as a child.

Billie was born on December 18, 2001, in Highland Park, a neighborhood a few miles northeast of downtown Los Angeles. In the 1990s it had appealed to people living on a budget, like Billie's parents, who were willing to brave an area with a high crime rate; but twenty-first-century gentrification changed the vibe. The Highland Park that Billie grew up in still had an edge, but was increasingly full of renovated houses and new bars, coffee shops, music venues, and restaurants. By 2019 *Time Out* magazine was featuring it as one of the top-ten coolest neighborhoods on the planet!

Here Billie Eilish Pirate Baird O'Connell entered the world. Eilish was originally going to be her first name (her parents had liked it since hearing it on a documentary about Irish conjoined twins), but when her maternal grandfather, Bill, died shortly before she was born, she was named Billie in his memory. Meanwhile, the fabulous Pirate moniker was insisted upon by her then four-year-old brother, Finneas. Baird came from her mother, Maggie Baird, and her father, Patrick O'Connell, provided the last name.

Maggie and Patrick were actors. They had met back in 1984 when they were both working on a play in Alaska, moved to LA in 1991 in order to find TV and movie opportunities, and were married in 1995. They were clearly talented—both had performed on Broadway in New York—but show business is a tough world. Although Maggie appeared on *Friends* and *Curb Your Enthusiasm* and joined the comedy troupe the Groundlings (where she appeared alongside Will Ferrell, Kristen Wiig, and Melissa McCarthy), and Patrick had parts in *The West Wing* and *Iron Man*, these roles were minor and short-lived.

It is often assumed that growing up in LA with actor parents, Billie had a privileged and affluent upbringing. However, nothing could be further from the truth. Long periods of unemployment are a regular occurrence for so many actors, and Maggie had to fall back on teaching jobs, while Patrick earned money through his carpentry skills or as a home repairer. They even renovated a house across the street from their own to sell and make a little money.

The house they bought in Highland Park is the one Billie grew up in and still calls home. It is a cozy, two-bedroom bungalow with a slightly chaotic but incredibly homey feel. Paintings, art created by members of the family, photographs, and handwritten notes adorn the walls; the shelves creak with books; and musical instruments lie everywhere. The house has three pianos, including a grand piano that Patrick managed to find for free online. Outside, the yard has a handmade tree house, a tire swing, and a patch of grass—everything a young child might need.

To complete the scene of domestic bliss, they were joined by two rescue pets: Misha, a black cat with a white "scarf" and a tabby face, and Pepper, a cute black-and-white pit bull mix with a black patch over one eye. Pepper can be seen alongside Billie in many photographs and seems particularly fond of licking her face. One picture, taken when Billie was around seven, shows the whole family all sporting a Pepper-style eye patch.

Two bedrooms were plenty for the young family. For many years they all slept together in one room. When Finneas turned ten, he got his own room, but soon, when Billie needed her own space too, the arrangement became problematic. Typically, in a family focused on the happiness of the children, the parents gave up their room and slept on a futon behind the piano in the living room. It was just a matter of priorities.

Making music and singing together was a permanent feature in the house.

They might have had little money, but on the plus side Maggie and Patrick had plenty of time for their children. They created an atmosphere of warmth and freedom for Finneas and Billie, often built around their own passions for music and performance. Patrick played ukulele and piano, and Maggie ran songwriting workshops, even releasing her own country-music CD, called *We Sail*, in 2009.

Making music and singing together was a permanent feature in the house. They would listen and sing along to Patrick's varied mixtapes, which threw together Green Day, the Beatles, Avril Lavigne, Linkin Park, ABBA, and others. On "Carpool Karaoke," Billie picked up the ukulele to play "I Will" by the Beatles, a song she learned when she was six years old, and on YouTube there's a clip of her performance of the Beatles's "Happiness Is a Warm Gun" at the age of eleven. Billie recalls how "music trumped everything" in the house—even bedtime, because no one was sent to bed if they were playing any kind of music.

Billie certainly couldn't complain about her parents being strict. The only rule she has mentioned was not being allowed to drink soda. The desire to allow their children the utmost freedom was highlighted by Maggie and Patrick's decision to homeschool both Finneas and Billie. When Maggie was pregnant with Finneas in the early summer of 1997, the song "MMMBop" by Hanson was Number 1 in the charts. Hanson comprised three brothers from Tulsa, Oklahoma, who had been homeschooled. Reading about these talented kids, Patrick was taken with the way they had been allowed to follow their own interests, and although he and Maggie were bringing up a family in exciting LA and not the Southwest, they vowed to homeschool their children too.

In interview after interview, Billie credits her homeschooling for nurturing her independent and creative spirit. There was no school schedule to follow, so the siblings' days were taken up with whatever enthusiasms they had. Although Billie learned enough to pass the equivalent of her high-school graduation at fifteen, much of her time was taken up with art, music, and other creative projects. She loved to make costumes and work on craft projects and, as she got older, would set up a camera in the backyard and star in her own mini movies. She admits she loved being photographed and filmed, and once harbored ambitions of being a model.

Billie credits her homeschooling for nurturing her independent and creative spirit.

Finneas had already followed in his parents' footsteps and set out on a career as an actor. At fourteen he played opposite Cameron Diaz in the movie *Bad Teacher*. Two years later, he starred in the independent film *Life Inside Out* (cowritten by his mother) and appeared in two episodes of *Glee*. Billie would have her own opportunities to act but spurned them. "I went on, like, two auditions," she told *Rolling Stone* magazine. "So lame. This creepy, cold room. All these kids that looked exactly the same. Most actor kids are psychopaths." She

Being homeschooled with her brother meant that Billie and Finneas weren't just siblings but best friends too.

did, however, enjoy recording background dialogue for movies with a bunch of other kids. You'll never pick her out, but her voice is there on *Diary of a Wimpy Kid*, *Ramona and Beezus*, and *X-Men*.

Being homeschooled with her brother meant that Billie and Finneas weren't just siblings but best friends too—a relationship so strong it has endured all the tribulations of songwriting, recording, and touring together. However, it wasn't a solitary life. Homeschooling was popular in LA, and the families formed a community providing friendship and support. There would be regular get-togethers and performances by the children. Once a week, parents would lead classes in a variety of subjects, such as cooking or sewing, and Billie took a songwriting class run by her mother. Maggie was an accomplished tutor; she taught the children how to begin writing a song, but gave them free reign by setting projects that would fire their imaginations. At eleven, Billie began songwriting in earnest and over the next few years surprised friends and adults with songs that showed great sophistication.

Billie and Finneas were also receiving a musical education at the LA Children's Chorus (LACC). She joined when she was eight years old and became a valued member of the group, only leaving when she was fifteen. Founded in the late 1980s, the chorus established an international reputation for its bel canto style of singing, which emphasizes smooth transitions across the vocal range. Billie credits the LACC with giving her the perfect

Inspired by the films of Shirley Temple, the dancing child star of the 1930s, she started tap lessons.

grounding as a singer, not only teaching her technique and how to look after her voice but also how to read and write music.

At the same time she was also learning to dance. Inspired by the films of Shirley Temple, the dancing child star of the 1930s, she started tap lessons. By the time she was eight, she was learning ballet and jazz too, and then she progressed to hip-hop and contemporary dance. Billie displayed real talent, joining a competitive dance company at twelve and enrolling in a number of classes, often with much older and more experienced dancers. We will never know how far she could have taken these skills, though, because within a year injury had forced her to focus her energies elsewhere.

Away from performance, Billie had developed another passion: horses. Her parents had saved money to pay for her to spend a week learning to ride at a local stable, but couldn't afford to pay for regular lessons. So Billie worked—mucking out, grooming, or helping with children's parties—in exchange for riding time. This lasted a couple of years, long enough for Billie to ride regularly on a beautiful black mare named Jackie O.

Despite paying her way, Billie was self-conscious around the rich girls who frequented the stable. When a wealthier girl was given Jackie O to ride ahead of Billie, it became all too much and she quit. She loved that horse, and although she didn't ride, she continued to visit the stable to spend time with her. Horses have remained a part of Billie's life, an escape from the pressures of fame and work. On tour, whenever she gets the opportunity, such as on the beach in Auckland, New Zealand, or at a country club outside Glasgow, Scotland, you will find her smiling and contented, riding horses.

BILLIE'S INSPIRATIONS

When Billie was twelve years old she was watching the music video to Aurora's "Runaway" and it all fell into place. That, she decided there and then, was what she wanted to do. Whether she would be successful and where it would take her, she didn't care. Those looking for similarities with the Norwegian singer can point to the fact that she wrote "Runaway" when she was twelve, but the clear voice and lo-fi synth backing were obviously something a young Billie could emulate. Years later, Aurora would return the love, saying of Billie, "I think the world needs more artists who just do what they want. She uses her voice in such a cool way."

Inevitably, Billie is compared to virtually every young female singer ever, especially those she has picked out as personal favorites—Amy Winehouse, Marina Diamandis, Halsey, Melanie Martinez, and even 1950s singer Peggy Lee. Lana Del Rey is perhaps the most obvious match—Billie once described her "Off to the Races" as the "most badass song I've ever heard in my life." It is clear that Del Rey's vocal range, phrasing and delivery, as well as her authenticity and ability to find beauty in sadness, were a major influence. Billie, however, rejects close comparisons with the acclaimed singer. "I don't want to hear that Billie Eilish is the new Lana Del Rey," she told the *Los Angeles Times* in 2019. "Do not disrespect Lana like that! That woman has made her brand so perfect for her whole career and shouldn't have to hear that."

Another name spoken alongside Billie's is that of New Zealand-born singer Lorde. Both of them had viral hits on SoundCloud at a young age, although Lorde's 2013 track "Royals" became a chart hit just months later. They share minimalist instrumental backing, sharp lyric writing (some might mistake "We're driving Cadillacs in our dreams" for a Billie Eilish line), and a hip-hop influence. Lorde's production is also heavy on vocal layers, while her singing has been called restrained, hushed, and haunting—terms often used to describe Billie's vocal style. However, for all the characteristics they share, they are totally different in many more ways, and as their careers developed, they have both proved that they are unique artists who stand on their own merits.

For all the liberal parenting, homeschooling, and precocious performances, Billie had a recognizably normal childhood. She rode her Razor scooter up and down the block, played with other children, and watched TV and movies. As she got older, she plastered her bedroom walls with pictures of Justin Bieber, worried about her appearance, obsessed over boys, and hung out with her friends in Starbucks. One of them, Zoe Donahoe, who was pictured with Billie back when they were five, can still be seen accompanying her "lil sister" on tours over ten years later. The other constant was Finneas. While he was now in his late teens and had his own pursuits, he continued to enjoy making music with his sibling. As his room increasingly came to resemble a recording studio, she could often be found watching him work and trying out her own songs.

Her life in Highland Park contributed to Billie developing the talent and personality to be a star at such a young age. Being exposed to a wide range of music, encouraged to play and sing her own songs, and given opportunities to perform clearly prepared her for a life as a musician. While homeschooling might not be for everyone, Billie seems to have thrived on the lack of control, routine, and peer pressure. She pins the fact that she puts such little stock in what others think of her down to not having to worry about her popularity among her classmates.

For all the liberal parenting, homeschooling, and precocious performances, Billie had a recognizably normal childhood.

However, from the age of thirteen, Billie's childhood started to change. It was invaded by external forces: music industry executives, promoters, managers, musicians, and fans. Many young people would have found it overwhelming. Billie was more prepared than most. Her upbringing had given her a rare confidence, a maturity beyond her years, a family that provided comfort and security, and, as the world would soon discover, considerable talent.

CHAPTER TWO
OVERNIGHT SENSATION

The story is now part of pop history, set to be retold a million times.

It's a fairy tale about a thirteen-year-old girl who went to bed a nobody and woke up a star. And while that sounds like a Disney movie plot, it really isn't too far from the truth. Billie Eilish was just a normal teenager who happened to post a song online, and Billie herself admits that when the song went viral, everything changed so suddenly it was difficult to take in. She just went along with it, loving every moment.

Back in the autumn of 2015, if any member of the O'Connell family seemed destined to be a star it was Billie's eighteen-year-old brother, Finneas, whose acting career was taking off. He had followed appearances in the movie *Bad Teacher* with TV roles, including a major part in the final season of *Glee,* which had been broadcast early in 2015. At the same time his band, the Slightlys, were winning friends and acclaim in Los Angeles. They had played in front of ten thousand people in the Santa Monica Pier Twilight Concert Series and an *LA Weekly* article in October 2014 had hinted that they might be "the next big thing."

Thirteen-year-old Billie was content to bask in her brother's success. After becoming disheartened by a disastrous audition, she had rejected the idea of following her parents and brother into the acting game, and by this time, much of her creative energy was directed toward dance. Billie's early enthusiasm for tap had grown into a love of all kinds of dance—and even now when she talks about dancing, it's clear she adores the freedom it gives her to express herself. At thirteen she was attending the Revolution Dance Center (RDC) in LA, where she spent up to eleven hours a week in the dance studio, concentrating on learning contemporary, lyrical, and hip-hop styles, and performing in regular competitions. Billie seemed set to become a dancer.

She still loved to sing, though. In fact, it was impossible *not* to sing in such a musical household. She would sing the songs her parents played, songs she loved herself, and songs she or Finneas had written. Through the bedroom wall, she could hear Finneas writing and recording music on Logic Pro at his workstation, and she knew his songs almost as well as he did. Billie would join him too, adding her soft, melodic voice to his compositions, harmonizing, and even trying out her own songs.

On August 1, 2015 (the day after Finneas's eighteenth birthday), they uploaded one of their collaborations to SoundCloud, the online platform for sharing and discovering original music. The song was titled "sHE's brOKen," with "HE's OK" standing out in capital letters and contrasting with the sentiment of the title. Billie must have been aware of the "sHE beLIEveD" meme (with "HE LIED" picked out in the same way) that had been popular across the web since 2012, but nevertheless, it was a smart variation on the

> # She still loved to sing, though. In fact, it was impossible *not* to sing in such a musical household.

theme. The lyrics painted a straightforward "end of relationship" picture to a simple backing track (enhanced by a few production gimmicks courtesy of Finneas), with Billie providing a sweet and tuneful vocal. You can certainly tell it is Billie, but there is none of the ethereal quality or even the candy-coated whispers of her later hits.

On September 14, another track appeared on SoundCloud. Billie says that "Fingers Crossed" was the first song she wrote and that she didn't like it at the time but just felt like uploading it. In a songwriting class, her mother had asked her to

Billie has said she intended to write about the zombie apocalypse, but somehow it came out as an anguish-filled love song.

watch a TV movie or show and note down any titles, names, or dialogue that would sit well in a song. Billie turned to her favorite show, *The Walking Dead*, and the zombie drama series provided lyrics such as "Everybody makes it 'til they don't" and "Too far gone," the title of one episode. Billie has since said she intended to write about the zombie apocalypse, but somehow it came out as an anguish-filled love song.

"Fingers Crossed" was different from the first song she had posted. Billie sings of longing and despair over a portentous track that's punctuated by a slow beat, sparse instrumentation, and drawn-out chords. Now there is an intimacy and poignancy to the vocals, with that feeling of Billie being incredibly close and yet so distant at the same time. It's a vocal style that would become familiar in the next couple of years, and many fans still rate the track highly.

BILLIE AND HIP-HOP

Billie was eleven years old and sitting on her bed listening to music. She shared her music library with Finneas and didn't know half the tracks on it. With her player on shuffle, "Heartbeat" by Childish Gambino, a song she had never heard before, came on, and she was awestruck. Here was a world she'd been missing. This is what she liked. Billie had met hip-hop.

At the time that "ocean eyes" hit SoundCloud in 2015, that same streaming platform had become a gold mine for those looking for innovative hip-hop acts. There was an exciting proliferation of punk rap, mumble rap, emo rap, and trap-influenced SoundCloud artists. Billie dived headfirst into this scene and came up loving Tyler, the Creator; XXXTentacion; Ski Mask the Slump God; Lil Pump; and others who were making DIY lo-fi tracks (often, like her and Finneas, in their own bedrooms).

Billie continued to have a voracious appetite for hip-hop. Like many teenagers, she loves Travis Scott, J. Cole, A$AP Rocky, and Drake (at one time she said "The Motto" was her favorite song) but also rappers like Denzel Curry, Earl Sweatshirt ("I wana have his kids," she tweeted in 2018), and Tierra Whack. She still takes great delight in discovering new talent and has promoted emerging artists such as Leikeli47, Smino, Moses, Dominic Fike, and British rapper Mehki Raine (formerly Crooks), who contributed vocals to "bury a friend."

Although she has never been a rap or hip-hop artist, so much about the Billie we see now is down to that genre. The clever wordplay in her lyrics, her F-you attitude, her outfits, her movements onstage, and the mosh-pit songs at her shows all have a connection to hip-hop. That said, she believes she's not alone. "Everyone needs to give hip-hop credit—everyone in the world right now," she told the *New York Times*. "Whatever you're doing, you've been influenced by hip-hop."

As you would expect, these tracks made very little impact at the time, with only a small number of plays registering on SoundCloud. Like thousands of kids (and adults), Billie and Finneas uploaded them for fun and intended to share them just with friends. They never dreamed that they would be played millions of times. Besides, Billie was busy dancing, working on her homeschool projects, and having fun. She even attended her first major concert that autumn, when she and Finneas went to see the hip-hop-inspired US rock band the Neighbourhood at the Shrine, a cavernous auditorium in LA. In 2019 she would return to the venue to play two sold-out concerts of her own.

What happened next would change Billie O'Connell's life forever. One of her dance teachers at RDC was Fred Diaz, a dancer and choreographer who had worked with several top artists, including Rihanna, Mariah Carey, and Jennifer Lopez. He knew of Billie and Finneas's songwriting efforts and had suggested he could choreograph a dance to one of their compositions. When she asked him what kind of song he had in mind, he mentioned "Station" by British singer Låpsley, a song they had recently danced to, and also alluded to a tune he had overheard her humming in class. She knew the song immediately.

It was one of her brother's, which she had heard through the bedroom wall and sung along to—and which had been going round and round in her head for the last couple of weeks. It was called "ocean eyes," and Finneas had originally written it for the Slightlys.

Although she didn't know it yet, Billie's career as a pop star had begun.

The band had already performed "ocean eyes," but Finneas suspected it might be perfect for Billie. She had been having a hard time with a boy she was obsessed with, and he sensed she would identify with it. He was right. Billie felt he had looked into her heart when he wrote the words—as if he had written it for her. When Billie sang along, it fit perfectly. She gave it a depth of feeling that it had never had before.

At the same time, Billie was thinking about the song as a dance track and how it could best suit a contemporary dance choreography. The siblings worked on the track together in Finneas's tiny bedroom studio, Billie sitting cross-legged on the bed while her brother sat at the computer. They worked on the tempo and arrangement (Finneas recalls how they agreed on everything about the song—which would not always be the case) and, having finished the recording, listened back to it and realized they had created something they could be really proud of. They uploaded the track to SoundCloud with a free download button for Fred Diaz. It was November 18, 2015, and although she didn't know it yet, Billie's career as a pop star had begun.

The next day Billie was in Starbucks, sheltering from the cold between dance classes, when she received a call from Finneas (Billie admits it may have been a couple of days later, but the overnight story is so much more dramatic!). He told her that the song had received a thousand plays on SoundCloud. They were both astounded. Of course, their friends would have been supportive and spread the word, but there was no way they knew that many people! Billie recalls that their ridiculously excited call went on so long that she ended up having to run to get to her next class in time—with a huge grin on her face.

Billie had taken her first two names as a stage name, so it may have been Billie O'Connell who uploaded the track, but as "ocean eyes" registered more and more plays, it was Billie Eilish who was rapidly gaining recognition. If you have ever uploaded a song, picture, or video online, you know how difficult it is to get likes or hits from outside your own circle, so you can probably imagine the disbelief and joy Billie and Finneas felt at the success of their song—and that was without any marketing or publicity. However, this was a well-crafted, excellently produced, and flawlessly sung track. It was going viral because it was a compelling and incredibly catchy song.

The three-and-a-half-minute "ocean eyes" is a dreamy ballad built on a minimal backing of soft percussion and electronic beats. The lyrics tell of an intense love and use metaphors ranging from blindness to burning cities to convey emotions from deep calm to immense agitation. The key to its appeal really is in Billie's singing. Her voice already sounds more mature than in her previous tracks and you can hear the influence of Lana Del Rey, Aurora, and Låpsley. Her vocals are strong and clear, but through her soprano voice and intense phrasing, they carry a fragility and sensitivity that conveys a powerful emotion.

Against all the odds, "ocean eyes" continued to get noticed.

This is all emphasized by the layering of her voice, which gives the whole song a heartrending, sad, and haunting quality.

For an unknown artist with no record-company backing it was an amazing release, but its chance of standing out among the millions of tracks on SoundCloud was miniscule. However, against all the odds, "ocean eyes" continued to get noticed. Within a week, the LA-based music blog *Free Bike Valet*, already friends of the Slightlys, had picked up on it, describing the track as "a hypnotic trip-pop smash built on delicate digi-beats, surreal synth effects and Eilish's angelically soft vox," while Californian music tastemakers Blah Blah Blah Science picked out Billie's "very graceful high-angelic stunning-dreamy harmonic vocals." It also began getting airplay on KCRW, a public radio station in nearby Santa Monica, where it had been discovered by their DJ, Jason Kramer.

The real game changer was a man named Chad Hillard, who claims to have spotted the track when it had just a hundred or so plays. Chad runs Hillydilly, a respected and influential website dedicated to unearthing new music, which "discovered" Lorde and Låpsley. With Hillydilly's recommendation and an article praising both "ocean eyes" and "Fingers Crossed," Billie was on her way. Six months later, she would acknowledge the importance of their backing when she wrote on Facebook: "Hillydilly.com started it all. Thank you for everything Michael Enwright [who wrote the article], Chad Hillard, I love you."

Within a couple of weeks, remixes of the track were appearing on SoundCloud too. Up-and-coming producer Cautious Clay and Justin Bieber's "Boyfriend" cowriter Blackbear both posted versions, but the standout and most popular was by an English songwriter and producer, Arron Davey, who works under the name Astronomyy. His remix emerged at the end of November 2015, and it surprised even Billie.

He messaged her on Instagram asking for the lyrics. She gave them to him, and the next thing she knew the remix had appeared on the site. Astronomyy claims he heard the track one night and immediately spent the next six hours working on it. His version doubles up on the haunting percussion and piercing vocals, and adds a subaquatic feel that heightens the already chilling atmospheric qualities of the song. For many, it was the best production of the song yet and, created by an artist whose own

> # Billie was naturally astounded and unprepared for the response to the track.

tracks had gathered millions of plays, it introduced "ocean eyes" to thousands more listeners.

Billie was naturally astounded and unprepared for the response to the track. Fortunately, through the Slightlys, Finneas had become friends with Danny Rukasin, a manager involved in the LA band scene. Rukasin immediately understood what was happening with "ocean eyes" and knew that a young girl like Billie—in fact, anyone—would be struggling to deal with the success. The day after it went viral, he offered to help and went to their home to meet with not only Billie but with Finneas and their parents too. He was eager to find out whether Billie was set on being a musician or if she was just happy with the attention the song was getting. It didn't take him long to realize she had already thought this through and had a clear idea of how she wanted to present herself to the world.

Dance was an important part of Billie's vision. She considered herself a dancer as much as, or even more than, a singer. As promised, Fred had choreographed a dance to "ocean eyes," but Billie got to work on it for just two days. She was in a hip-hop class with an older group when she ruptured the growth plate in her hip. Her dancing days weren't finished, but they were on ice for the time being. Fortunately, she had another passion to fall back on and it was gathering steam.

As Billie celebrated her fourteenth birthday on December 18, 2015, it must have been difficult to take it all in. "Ocean eyes" had now garnered over 150,000 plays, she was featured regularly in new music articles online, and she was receiving all kinds of offers. The input of entertainment-industry-savvy parents, a brother who was himself only just dipping his toes in the LA music scene, and a friendly local manager were all incredibly welcome, but if Billie was going to build on this success—and do it her own way—she was going to need more help, quickly.

CHAPTER THREE
THE REAL DEAL

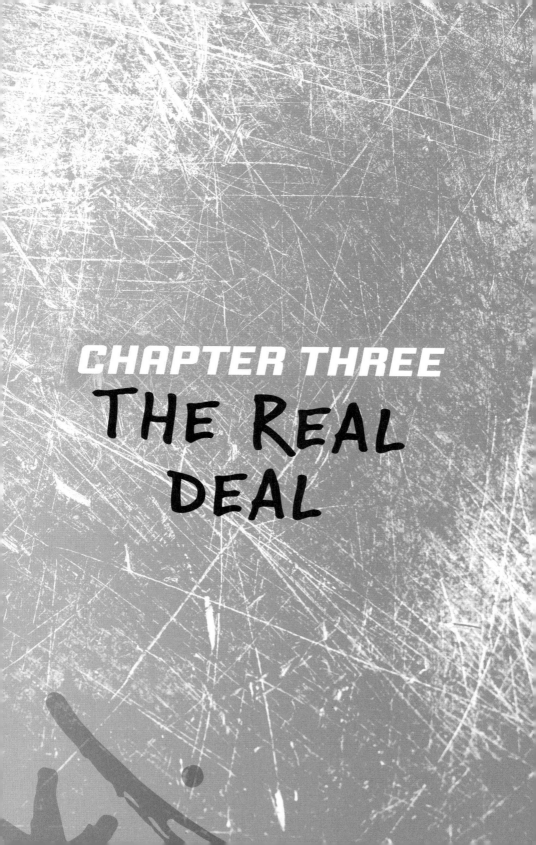

For some, finding the truly authentic pop star is the holy grail of modern music.

They immediately discount anyone who emerges from talent shows such as *X-Factor* or *America's Got Talent*, or anyone who is styled and prepped for stardom from an early age, like Britney Spears, Christina Aguilera, or the Jonas Brothers. Others are dismissed as "industry plants"—Ed Sheeran and Justin Bieber are often cited as examples—a term that implies a person is pretending to have made it through sheer talent when really they had a record company or industry figures behind them. If you can fake authenticity, cynics say, you're the real deal!

The truth is, in a world of global charts, streaming sites, and mega promotions, it is impossible to break through to the general public without some serious backing. Some people are molded by producers, publicists, and stylists from a young age, while others are discovered and identified as potential stars. By January 2016, "ocean eyes" had put Billie Eilish, now fourteen, in both categories: young enough to be turned into a star and talented enough to be taken under a company's wing.

She was young enough to be turned into a star and talented enough to be taken under a company's wing.

Some have hung the "industry plant" tag on Billie as she had parents in the entertainment industry, a brother in the music business, and even a manager offering help, but that is to completely ignore the fact that these people were all minor players without any clout. They did, however, know enough about the business to advise Billie to tread carefully. She knew her own mind, and if she was going to be successful, it was going to be on her own terms—but she would still need money and know-how.

Enter Denzyl Feigelson. He (along with Saul Klein, the money man behind Songkick, last.fm, and SoundCloud) had just set up Platoon, a company that he hoped would supply "a platform for fearless creatives." Feigelson had worked in the music business since the 1980s and had always championed independent, unsigned talent, even creating Artists Without A Label (AWAL), a business helping acts distribute their own CDs. As the twenty-first century progressed, he had been instrumental in setting up Apple Music and the iTunes Festival. He had seen which way the wind was blowing and especially how SoundCloud, Spotify, and iTunes had radically reshaped the music industry.

Platoon reached out to artists like Billie who were making a splash on these sites. They offered the services traditionally supplied by record companies, such as marketing and promotion, video production, and recording studios, without tying artists to long-term contracts, taking a share of song rights or, perhaps most importantly for Billie, restricting their creative freedom. They were already helping their first signing, English singer-songwriter Jorja Smith, release a single, "Blue Lights," on her own label and were the perfect fit for the fiercely independent Billie.

As Billie signed up with Platoon in January 2016, the new year continued where the old had left off, with "ocean eyes" picking up ever more plays. It was boosted by yet another remix, this time by DJ and producer Goldhouse, who had won considerable acclaim already for his Lady Gaga and Sam Smith remixes. His version gave "ocean eyes" a completely different vibe: upbeat with added instrumentation creating a trop-house feel (very much the thing in early 2016). The track was now a club hit, too, and Billie clearly loved it, remarking on Facebook, "This remix is LIT!"

Meanwhile, Billie and Finneas were working on new songs. On January 12, Billie's Facebook post read, "Makin bangers with Cheat Codes today" along with a photo of her and Trevor Dahl from the electronic music trio. Fellow LA residents Cheat Codes were also on their way up. They had had success with their track "Visions" six months before "ocean eyes" and had followed it with another viral hit, "Adventure," which earned them

The track was now a club hit, and Billie clearly loved it, remarking on Facebook, "This remix is LIT!"

a slot as support on a Chainsmokers tour. Billie and Finneas would record two tracks (one of theirs and one of the Cheat Codes's) with them. However, in February, Cheat Codes released "Sex" with Dutch trio Kriss Kross Amsterdam, which immediately went super viral, gaining millions of plays around the world. As Cheat Codes's career took off, the tracks they had recorded with Billie were shelved and have still not seen the light of day.

All that most of those streaming "ocean eyes" knew of Billie was that she was thirteen when she recorded the track and that she worked with her brother. Many might also have seen a picture accompanying the song on SoundCloud, a striking black-and-white photo of a young girl looking two or three years older than thirteen. In it, Billie stared past the camera, her long blonde hair with dark roots falling completely over one eye.

Early in March a select few—many of whom were friends or people who knew Billie already—witnessed her first performance. It took place in a small club called the Hi Hat that had only recently opened just around the corner from her house in Highland Park. Playing as a support act to the UK band Mt. Wolf, Billie and Finneas took to the stage dressed mainly in black (Billie in leggings, T-shirt, and a jacket), and although there was only an audience of around fifty people, the

The video successfully matches the intensity of the song because of Billie's extraordinary ability to create drama from nothing.

general feeling was that they blew them all away.

Later that month, the world was to get to know Billie a lot better. On March 24, 2016, the video to "ocean eyes" was released. It had been shot in December 2015 by Megan Thompson, an LA director who had worked with interesting indie acts such as Hands Like Houses and Astronautalis. Shot at the Eilish home, the video comprised a simple continuous shot of Billie facing the camera and standing in front of a blue flowing curtain.

The video successfully matches the intensity of the song because of Billie's extraordinary ability to create drama from nothing, to fill the screen with her presence and convey such powerful emotion through her eyes and small hand movements. She wears a simple black top and her hair, still blonde with dark roots, has wet-look ends that fall below her shoulders. She has pronounced black under-eye liner, shiny red-brown mascara, and looks conventionally pretty yet "interesting." Billie herself wasn't impressed, though, later saying, "It was the day after my birthday that we shot this. I had just turned 14. They put makeup on me that I did not want, and they did my hair very f***ing weird."

Since "ocean eyes" Billie and Finneas had continued to work

on songs old and new. On June 23, seven months after that fateful release, they dropped "Six Feet Under," a song they had been working on for some time. Thanks to the Platoon deal, it not only appeared on SoundCloud but also enjoyed a worldwide digital release on iTunes, Spotify, Tidal, and Amazon. The lyrics, music, and production on "Six Feet Under" were Finneas's work, but the performance is all Billie. It follows "ocean eyes" in the ethereal, breathless, and intense singing elucidating every word over a sparse synth backing track, but Billie stretches herself, especially when she holds the note on "bloom." Once again, Finneas's lines are simple, but cut to the quick with short phrases and deft metaphor.

Although it didn't immediately take off in the way "ocean eyes" had, the single did strengthen Billie's core following, and some of those fans were in positions of influence and had popular playlists on Spotify. Most notable of all was Apple Music Beats 1 radio presenter Zane Lowe, who premiered "Six Feet Under" on his show, describing the single as "absolutely incredible" and Billie as "an amazing new talent." Just days after release the song was also featured in the soundtrack to the incredibly popular teen thriller series *Pretty Little Liars*, which also gave it a real boost.

TYLER, THE CREATOR

In the early years of her fame there weren't many interviews with Billie when she didn't name Tyler, the Creator as her favorite artist and biggest influence. Tyler was the founder of the underground rap group Odd Future (whose members have included Frank Ocean and Earl Sweatshirt) but also built a successful solo career.

His break came in 2011 with a viral YouTube video for his single "Yonkers" and an erratic, hyperactive performance on *Late Night with Jimmy Fallon*. His debut album, *Goblin*, reached Number 5 in the Hot 100 and his subsequent albums, *Wolf* (2013), *Cherry Bomb* (2015), and *Flower Boy* (2017), did progressively better until 2019's *Igor* hit the top of the charts and won a 2020 GRAMMY for best rap album.

Billie first came across Tyler in 2013 when she was working at the stables, helping out with a camp for younger children. A fellow helper asked if she liked him and was surprised Billie hadn't even heard of him as he was her profile picture (she just thought he looked cool). They listened to his hit "Tamale" as the five-year-olds rode past, and Billie was hooked. She was beginning to get into hip-hop, but it was no surprise that she saw something special in Tyler, the Creator. His songs have many allusions to horror and dark themes, and he isn't afraid to explore his own mental frailties. Remind you of anyone?

Aside from the fact that both are Angelinos (although from opposite sides of the city), there is an obvious connection between Billie and Tyler in that they share a creative impulse that goes beyond music. Tyler has always created his own artwork, directs his own videos, and exerts creative control over all aspects of his recordings and performance. Early in his career he also set up a clothing brand called Golf Wang to sell his own colorful, vibrant, and occasionally controversial streetwear, shoes, and skateboard designs.

Billie first met Tyler when she visited his Golf Wang shop in LA and was invited to hang out with him in the back room, and she remains a massive fan, citing him as a true genius. In a 2019 interview with Zane Lowe, Tyler revealed that he loved her music, too, and that he would like to collaborate with her. Billie quickly responded on Instagram, saying, "i would never in a billion years have thought these words would come out of this mans mouth. wow. i would be nothing without you tyler. everyone knows it."

Things were now gathering pace. By August 2016, Billie had signed to Darkroom, an artist management company and label. Darkroom was run by twenty-eight-year-old Justin Lubliner, who had recently linked up with Interscope Records, a major record label whose roster included Lady Gaga and Lana Del Rey. Lubliner's first signing was an electronic dance-music artist called Gryffin, but after hearing "ocean eyes" he was determined to make Billie the next Darkroom artist. "Within one second of hearing it and seeing her photo, it just clicked," he told *Hits Daily Double* website. "I felt like this was the artist that I'd been searching for my entire career. I was going to make sure I did everything possible to work with her."

> **Billie directed her own video for "Six Feet Under."**

Lubliner and Billie seemed to share a vision based around her identity, visual creativity, and performances. They wanted to avoid the conventional strategy of launching new artists through a heavily promoted and hopefully hit single (such as Katy Perry's "I Kissed a Girl" or Iggy Azalea's "Fancy") and, instead, were determined to build Billie's profile through a series of varied releases, presenting her unique persona, individual aesthetic, and enormous talent.

Disappointed with the "ocean eyes" video, Billie directed her own video for "Six Feet Under," which was edited by her mother. It featured clips of smoke balls set off in front of the fence at her house, which filled the backyard with red, blue, and yellow smoke. It was interesting and artful, and so was Billie, but many fans wanted to see her performing it live.

They didn't have to wait long. On August 8, she and Finneas performed the song at an intimate venue in Los Angeles for Sofar Sounds, a project promoting live performances by new artists. Onstage, Finneas sat at the keyboard in a light brown T-shirt and jacket with Billie sitting next to him on a stool. Her hair was tied back in a casual ponytail, and she wore a white sweatshirt paired with a flared, pleated, short white skirt. This time, she had on minimal makeup and big hooped silver earrings. She was still only fourteen, and yet she sang with such grace and confidence to Finneas's stripped-back piano accompaniment. By the end of the month a video had been uploaded to YouTube, and it was clear to anyone watching that here was a true star in the making.

As "Six Feet Under" continued to garner plays, soon reaching the one million mark, and versions of "ocean eyes" surpassed twenty million, Billie went on the road. The Rickshaw Stop was still in California, but it was out in San Francisco. There Billie supported another emerging solo artist, Michl. Backed by Finneas as well as a bassist and a drummer on an electric kit, Billie played a set that included

It was clear to anyone watching that here was a true star in the making.

not only "ocean eyes" and "Six Feet Under," but also "bellyache," "hostage," "my boy," "party favor" (featuring Billie on ukulele), and the beautiful "True Blue," which, despite being a live-fan favorite, has yet to be recorded.

Heartfelt lyrics about heartache and damaged indifference age her well beyond fourteen years old.

Interestingly, photos of the concert reveal a pre-stylist Billie displaying a penchant for baggy clothes as she stands at the mic wearing an oversized white shirt and casual gray pants, with her long blonde hair now parted off-center. The huge, unmissable crosses marker-penned on her hands mark her out as an underage guest at the club, but she clearly gave a mature performance. A review by the *Sweet Sound Bites* blog remarked how her "heartfelt lyrics about heartache and damaged indifference age her well beyond fourteen years old."

Back in Los Angeles, Billie and the band played another gig, this time opening for Canadian electronic dream-pop outfit Mu at Tenants of the Trees, a cocktail-bar venue in the Silver Lake area of the city. Although playing as a support act in small venues, Billie was getting noticed. In late September she was invited to *Teen Vogue*'s Young Hollywood celebration event in Malibu, California, taking her place in the photo-call dressed in a modest green T-shirt dress with a matching pendant, wearing a camo baseball cap over her pigtails. Still only fourteen, she already looked comfortable and assured among Hollywood's going-places teenagers.

CHAPTER FOUR
BELLYACHE

It might have been a year late, but Billie finally got to perform Fred Diaz's choreography for "ocean eyes."

This was the original reason she had recorded the song, and she uploaded a "dance performance" video to YouTube in January 2017. Although she had spent the year injured and absent from the dance floor, Billie was determined to play her part, taking center stage in a fluid and emotional dance that did indeed perfectly match the mood of the song. Alongside her in the video were the friends she had loved dancing with in classes. That must have seemed a long time ago, though, before her life as a singer took off.

She was still only fourteen years old. She wasn't yet being recognized in the street, but she certainly had a growing presence online. Many of those getting in touch with her didn't realize how young she was and approached her like any adult musician. "It's insanely surreal. It's really hard to process everything when that much is going on," she told Dash Radio. "It's weird because I see my name—Billie Eilish—like Blackbear will tweet me and I don't realize it's me. I have to think, 'Oh, that's me that they are talking about, not just a name I am hearing.'"

In live performances Billie was growing in confidence. She was still opening for more established acts, but more and more people who were familiar with her material were showing up. Moreover, she could see how her songs were connecting with an audience, even moving some of them to tears. To someone who knew that same feeling from listening to other artists' music, this was truly amazing. "I wake up and can't believe people know that my work and my music exist," she said. The only problem was that the shows were taking place in venues that didn't admit under-eighteens or under-twenty-ones. From feedback and comments on social media, Billie and Finneas knew there was a groundswell of young teenagers who loved their music but couldn't access their live performances.

The deal with Interscope Records bore its first fruit on November 18 with the worldwide digital release of "ocean eyes" and the *Ocean Eyes—The Remixes* EP, which brought together the Astronomyy, Blackbear, Goldhouse, and Cautious Clay versions. These, along with the remixes of "Six Feet Under" from Jerry Folk, Gazzo, and BLU J (which were themselves released as an EP in February 2017) and the live appearances, kept the interest bubbling nicely.

With ongoing injuries keeping her dancing on hold, Billie had been directing her energies toward songwriting for the last year. She and Finneas had tried working with different producers and in various recording studios but always returned to his bedroom studio, deciding that the mood, comfort, and routines of their familiar setup were the most conducive for producing the sound she was looking for.

The first half of 2017 would see the fruition of this work in a series of singles, beginning with "bellyache" in February. The story of how "bellyache" was written says a lot about her creativity and imagination, and how her and her brother's minds work in sync. She has described how she was hanging out with Finneas and a couple of his friends, rehearsing for a show. They were jamming along on guitar and piano when Billie came up with the opening, a typical pop-song cliché about sitting alone with a mouthful of gum. Finneas added a line about the friends being in the back of the car. Then Billie hit on the evil and genius twist—the

From the outset Billie insisted that her imagination was enough to justify a song's lyrics.

narrator had killed them all. The siblings worked on the song from there, with Finneas contributing his own twist with the "bellyache" line giving the murderer a shocking nonchalance or naivety.

From the outset Billie insisted that her imagination was enough to justify a song's lyrics. Putting yourself into someone else's head—no matter how far-fetched—was perfectly acceptable if you had the creativity to carry it off. Nobody could insist you had to have experienced love or rejection yourself to write a song about romance, and you really didn't need to have killed anyone to pen a song about murder and guilt.

Surprisingly, with such dark and discomfiting lyrics, "bellyache" was Billie's most upbeat release to date. Although the characteristic synth chords and slow beats are still there, they are overridden by a strumming up-tempo acoustic guitar with a Latin sound that hovers on the brink of a summer ditty and even a dance break. Billie's voice is more forceful than ever but still portentous. It mirrors the mind of her character as it drifts from sing-along to irony to thoughtful and on to the turmoil of the "losing her mind" chorus.

"Bellyache" was not a massive chart hit. It wasn't intended to be. Following the Platoon and Darkroom plan, they were not chasing

She would wear clothes that looked uncomfortable and made an impression on people.

chart success but putting out authentic, unique tracks that would help establish Billie's identity. As *Billboard* wrote, "She [Billie] knows that a song like 'Bellyache' is going to get her more sideways glances than Top 40 airplay, and that's fine with her." Instead, the single reached Number 11 on both the US Bubbling Under Hot 100 Chart and the *Billboard* US Alternative Digital Song Sales Chart.

Billie's identity was also being influenced by a publicist, Alexandra Baker, who put her in touch with a stylist, Samantha Burkhart. Burkhart didn't create Billie's style, but she understood what Billie was about and was able to help. Growing up in LA was pretty cool for Billie, but she was one of the few who didn't love the Californian sun. The weather certainly wasn't ideal for someone who loved big, baggy garments, colorful outfits, and plenty of layers. She would wear clothes that looked uncomfortable and made an impression on people—even an unfavorable one. "Sometimes I'll wear four coats," she told *Vice* magazine. "I've worn pants on my arms; I wore camel pants on my arms as a shirt once." Burkhart describes how when she first met Billie, the then fourteen-year-old was wearing a giant white fluffy jacket. It looked cool, but it was 95°F (35°C) in the street! Her job would be to help Billie develop her style and source more cool outfits for her.

The first evidence of this came in the video for "bellyache," a three-minute gem directed by Miles Cable and AJ Favicchio (known as Miles and AJ). Under a blazing hot sun in the Californian desert, Billie appears in a bright all-yellow outfit comprising a turtleneck sweater, overalls, and a jacket, finished with fishnet socks and white Converse high-tops. Although to many, this appeared to be Billie dressing up for the song's story, we would soon discover that this was in fact Billie dressing exactly how she wanted. As she pulled her wagon with garbage bags full of dollars along the empty road, she once again showed she was a natural performer. Not required to sing along, she acted out the role of fugitive killer-thief with humor, anguish, indifference, and even some short dance moves, leading the viewer delightfully into the twist as she walks straight into a waiting police officer.

Billie said of the track that she didn't need that many people to care: she liked it and that was what was important. Even though the radio play wasn't forthcoming, critics seemed to love it. Digital Journal wrote that "all of the hype she is getting from music critics is based on talent and merit. Eilish deserves to become the next big female star in pop music." In the UK, the BBC said that "bellyache" was "the pop equivalent of a Tarantino movie— finding comic absurdity in the midst of eye-popping gore."

"Bellyache" would mark the start of a new phase of Billie's career. From playing the odd concert, working on songs with Finneas and other songwriters, and living like a normal teenager, life was about to change gear. It began with a festival. In a few years, she would be a festival queen, playing at the world's biggest events, but the CRSSD Festival in San Diego in early March 2017 was the first. Focusing on underground electronic music, this festival was a good fit for Billie, who took to the stage in a shiny pink three-piece outfit augmented with a black bustier worn outside her shirt. It was early on the first day, and there were just a handful of people sitting on the grass to watch her. However, two of them were singing along to the chorus of "ocean eyes." It was the first time this had ever happened, and she couldn't help but wonder how it would feel to have a massive audience all singing along.

CRSSD proved to be a warm-up for an altogether bigger festival. A music, film, and arts festival, SXSW in Austin, Texas, has grown every year since 1987, and hundreds of artists appear. In 2017, Lana Del Rey, Weezer, and the Wu-Tang Clan were among the headliners, but way down the list of acts came Billie Eilish. It was a great opportunity to play to music-industry figures, meet journalists and, of course, win over new fans. Billie would play as much as she could over a couple of days at the festival, including headlining Apple Music's artist-showcase event, where she was photographed with Kate Nash, Chloë Grace Moretz, and Bridgit Mendler. Also noteworthy was a gig Billie played on the patio of the La Zona Rosa venue before going inside to watch the main act, Vince Staples. "I wasn't feeling good," she said in a festival interview, "so I was just like, I'm gonna go mosh because I need to get it out, so I did." It wouldn't be too long before Vince would feature in her story.

Before March was over, Billie would have another boost. Netflix launched a TV series called *13 Reasons Why* based on a best-selling novel by Jay Asher. The series told a dark story of adolescent life and was an immediate hit, especially with teenage viewers. Part of the success of the show was due to the intense and haunting soundtrack from established acts such as Selena Gomez (the show's producer) and the Cure but also from new artists, including Lord Huron and the Japanese House. Online forums were busy fielding questions from viewers wanting to know who recorded specific contributions to the soundtrack. Often the answer was the as yet little-known Billie Eilish, singing a track called "Bored."

The soundtrack was released at the same time as the TV series and included "Bored," a track written (with input from Finneas) by established songwriting team Aron Forbes and Tim Anderson, who had previously worked with Banks and Halsey. The song, a bitter and self-assertive commentary on an uncaring lover set to a poignant synth backing, suited Billie perfectly. She delivers the lyrics in the same sweet, deadpan, but somehow loaded-with-emotion manner seen in the previous singles.

BILLIE THE TEENAGER

What has defined Billie Eilish more than anything else in interviews and articles written about her since 2015? Her voice? Her music? Her lyrics? Her clothes? All of those are regularly mentioned, but being a teenager trumps them all. She is never allowed to forget it; she is the star who has never bought a CD, who thought Bill and Hillary Clinton were siblings, who had never heard of Van Halen . . .

Over the years she has constantly fielded the "How does it feel?" question in the same straight way. "What's it like being fifteen?"

"Oh my God, I don't know," she responded to *Harper's Bazaar* in 2017. "It's the way that I feel. I've never been older. Ask me every single year and I'll give you the same answer." What is clear is that Billie has never felt the need to apologize for her youth. As a teen, her experience of the world is as valid as anyone's. When "ocean eyes" first became popular, few knew she was fourteen and the song stood on its own merits. Perhaps, in an ideal world, this is how she would have liked it to be forever, her age irrelevant to the quality of her music and art.

When forced, however, to be the spokesperson for her generation, she rises to the occasion. She was entitled to write about love or betrayal, she would argue, because young people experience these things too—often more acutely. "People underestimate the power of a young

mind that is new to everything and experiencing for the first time," she told the *NME* in 2019. "We're being ignored and it's so dumb. We know everything."

In her songwriting, Billie writes about her own world, but it is one she shares with millions of teenagers around the world. She writes of broken relationships, depression, fantasy, and even TV programs; all things they can identify with. Her initial fans might have been twentysomethings (and many still are), but teenagers took her to their hearts as one of them. It was only recently that she was an obsessive fan herself, her walls covered with Justin Bieber posters, and like her younger fans, she spilled every thought and emotion on Instagram and Twitter, and like them, she is learning from new experiences and constantly changing.

Reluctantly, Billie accepts that she is a role model for them and, especially when it comes to mental health, that she has a responsibility; she wants to be as supportive as possible. But what many teens admire in her is her straight-talking. As she told *Entertainment Weekly* in May 2019, "You have to be exactly what people love you for, even if that's a f***ing psycho—people like you, girl!"

The Billie Eilish train was in motion. In September 2019 she was invited to take part in a photoshoot for *Elle* magazine. Billie was featured in its annual "Women in Music" issue, as one of "19 women on the verge of star status." She was shot alongside American Apparel model-turned-singer Kacy Hill. Billie hugged the freckled Kanye West protégé from behind, her silver hair matching her $1,500 Paco Rabanne silver hoodie dress and $11,000 Tiffany necklace (along with necklaces of her own).

If you had to guess which of them was the hip-hop-influenced star, you'd have surely picked the chain-laden Eilish over Kacy Hill in her Stella McCartney check jacket.

Meanwhile, Billie and Finneas were busy in the studio rehearsing, tweaking their backlog of songs and getting them down on tape. "My sister @billieeilish gave one of the best vocal performances I've ever heard in the studio tonight," tweeted Finneas. He later replied to his own tweet to say that it was the night she sang the first verse of "my boy." And he wasn't the only one working on Billie's music. The songwriting and production duo Marian Hill had delivered a stunning remix of "bellyache." Retaining Billie's superb delivery, they wound down the acoustic guitar and introduced a bass-heavy synth feel that served to increase the drama and sinister tone. Not only did it introduce Billie to Marian Hill's not inconsiderable following, but the track also made Spotify's New Music Friday and Pop Remix playlists—each with thirty million followers.

The strategy that Platoon, Darkroom, and Interscope had drawn up with Billie was going exactly to plan. The drip-feed of singles, remixes, live performances, and interviews had continued to raise her profile. Since releasing "bellyache" she had gained over thirty-one thousand fans on Facebook—three times the increase of the previous three months—while Instagram and Spotify followers had grown similarly, fueled by the *13 Reasons Why* broadcast. What was perhaps more surprising was that this fifteen-year-old was such a refreshing persona in the pop world. She wrote lyrics at a level that belied her young age; she could perform with emotion, humor, and sincerity; she was developing an image that was unique, colorful, and recognizable; and, in interviews, she proved engaging and intelligent, while maintaining her identity as a teenager. If *Elle* had looked for just one woman on the verge of star status, they wouldn't have had to look much further than Billie Eilish . . .

CHAPTER FIVE
DONT SMILE

On June 24, 2017, Billie posted a message on Facebook that just read, "Finished the EP."

It must have been a great feeling. In virtually every interview she had done over the last year, she had said that she was impatient to get her music out. The songs that eventually appeared on the EP had been written a year or even eighteen months before, and it had been a long process. Billie complained that so much time had been wasted by her label trying to get her to work with established songwriters and producers. "They're all about eighty!" she exaggerated to emphasize her point.

These "octogenarians" might have created hit records, but Finneas and Billie had made "ocean eyes" with no help from anyone. She soon became frustrated at having to tactfully decline these guys' suggestions or politely persuade them to try her ideas, and she yearned for the easier and more open relationship she had with Finneas, where each of them just said what they thought. However, even when the label gave in and left Finneas and Billie alone in the studio, it still didn't seem right. Only when they returned to his bedroom did they achieve real progress on the EP.

The label executives were quickly learning that Billie might have been a young teenager, but she was also an artist who knew exactly what she wanted. Billie not only knew how she wanted her songs to sound, but she knew how she wanted to present them too. Even Finneas expressed surprise at how her vision for some of the songs seemed so different from his—even when he had written them. The point was perfectly illustrated by the video for "Bored."

The song is about being trapped in a relationship that's going nowhere, and other people might have filmed it with Billie acting all dreamy-eyed and soulful alongside some good-looking but doleful guy. Not Billie. She came up with the concept of climbing an endless ladder in a white space—a "timeless, anti-gravity space where no rules apply," she explained. All

Her sweet tones are undercut with venom and defiance.

in bright blue, outfitted in a hoodie, designer tracksuit, puffer jacket, and high-top Nikes, with her long silver hair, flawless skin, and pouting lips, Billie looks amazing.

The new EP would also follow the strategy of drip-feeding Billie's songs to an ever-curious public, with the tracks being dropped regularly until its release in early August. First up was "watch," a song that Finneas had written alone just a week or so after "ocean eyes" had been uploaded. To an upbeat synth track, a beat provided by the sound of a striking match and a killer chorus, Billie completely owns the vocals. Her sweet tones are undercut with venom and defiance. "I'll sit and watch your car burn with the fire that you started in me," she warns. And it sounds more than a little scary.

BILLIE AND TOURETTE'S SYNDROME

A YouTube video compilation appeared in late 2018. It had collected together moments from interviews over the years where Billie's eyebrows had twitched, her eyeballs jolted, or her neck had jerked. These tics were subtle and would generally have passed unnoticed at the time, but placed alongside one another they were unmistakable symptoms of Tourette's syndrome.

Many think of involuntary and compulsive swearing when they think of Tourette's, but such tics are much more common signs. Billie had been diagnosed with the syndrome at an early age and had largely been able to suppress any twitches when filmed. She hadn't ever mentioned it as she didn't want to be associated with the condition.

However, the video brought matters to a head, so Billie went on Instagram to explain. She says how, having grown up with it, she was used to the tics, and her friends and family think of it as part of her. More sadly, she hints at how problematic it can be: "HAVING them is a different type of misery," she writes and later in the post tells how suppressing the tics makes things worse once the moment has passed.

The way she dealt with the issue in such a matter-of-fact way, even admitting the videos were "low key funny," said so much about Billie's relationship with her supporters. She understood their curiosity and was determined to be as open as possible.

With the EP in the can, Billie was free to perform live again and it was time for her first headline show, but amazingly it took place over five thousand miles away from Highland Park, in London. The Courtyard Theatre holds only 250 people, and in just a few days it sold out to the curious and the already converted Billie Eilish fans in the UK capital. Accompanied only by Finneas on keyboards or acoustic guitar, Billie played a full set to an enthusiastic crowd who were happy to dance along. She was clearly still gaining confidence in her performance, but established a great rapport with her audience and must have been amazed, such a long way from home, to find them joining in with "ocean eyes." "I love traveling and that specific trip was a dream to me, especially since the show was sold out," she told *Decorated Youth* magazine. "I've never, never even had anything similar happen in my life so it was unbelievable." The experience clearly stayed with her as she would recall playing the gig when she was on the Glastonbury stage two years later.

At the Courtyard, as at every other gig when she'd played it, "COPYCAT" had been one of the best-received songs of the evening. Now it would receive a wider audience as the next of the list of tracks from the EP to drop. "COPYCAT" was Billie's

If "bellyache" was fiction, "COPYCAT" is personal. It is very much Billie keeping it real as she lays on the swag and attitude in a cold, calculated tone.

song. Her success had spawned a host of singers imitating her style, but the song was aimed at a particular girl who massively annoyed her by copying everything that she did. Billie described it as "the most honest song I have." It follows a familiar style of minimal beats and haunting synth—loose enough to turn the song into a noisy rock out in some live performances—but it is Billie's delivery and lyrics that make it stand out.

If "bellyache" was fiction, "COPYCAT" is personal. It is very much Billie keeping it real as she lays on the swag and attitude in a cold, calculated tone. Billie said she wrote it to go straight to the heart of her imitator. The curt and cutting phrases are full of ingenious wordplay and the lyrics twist and turn the listener inside out—right down to the "heartfelt" apology followed by the retro-teenage sucker punch, "Psych!" The

It's the perfect teenage-anguish song, addressing depression, insecurity, and body image.

whole song screams "don't mess with me," and you really feel you wouldn't want to.

But then, just a week later, comes a new track, the fifth single from the imminent EP, in which Billie reveals a self far from the assertive arrogance of "COPYCAT." "I just wish you could feel what you say," she sings at the beginning of "idontwannabeyouanymore." With more clever wordplay, she inverts the sense of the previous track. You want to be me so badly? Well guess what? I can't stand me. On Instagram, Billie promoted the new track, saying it was "a very inside of me song that has finally come out so if you'd like to hear deep inside my HEAD then GOO LISTEN."

"Idontwannabeyouanymore," with its soft piano, strings, and stop-start beat, has a jazzy feel to it, with Billie's vocals measured but always threatening to crack. She's putting her inner torment out there. Addressing her own image in the mirror, she sings of self-doubt and even self-loathing. In many ways it's the perfect teenage-anguish song, addressing depression, insecurity, and body image; but for Billie, now living her life in public, these emotions are magnified. "This song is from the perspective of me towards me," she said of the intensely personal track. "You are always you forever and that is terrifying . . ."

Another week, another track. The origins of "my boy" go back to one day when Billie ran into her brother's room and shouted, "My boy's being sus." Finneas laughed and said, "I'm going to use that," and they both sat down and wrote the song there and then. It's a song full of surprises. At first, it seems like another plinky-plonk jazz-styled song, but then it suddenly switches tempo to become a cool trip-hop number. It shapes up like a misused-girlfriend ballad, but emerges as a

She had written from her imagination, from deep within her own soul, and now from real-life experience.

self-assertive F-you tirade, and for all that the opening line is an attention grabber, the closing "If you want a good girl, then goodbye" is the ultimate kiss-off payofff.

With a handful of songs under her belt, Billie had already proved she was an incredibly versatile songwriter. She had written from her imagination, from deep within her own soul, and now from real-life experience. Those who knew Billie had a pretty good idea who she was writing about in "my boy" and made sure he heard it. Her friends told how he'd listened to it with his hood up and the strings pulled tight, hiding his face. Maybe it was a cruel exposé of a teenage romance gone wrong, but as least he'd inspired a pretty cool song.

For now, none of the tracks were bothering the mainstream charts, but Billie was building a healthy following. Over two hundred thousand fans were following her on Instagram, and "ocean eyes" had amassed more than fifteen million streams on Spotify and had featured on the soundtrack to the YA movie *Everything, Everything*. She was in demand for interviews, had begun to be recognized in the street, and was soon to embark on a sold-out headlining tour across the country. But first, there was the small matter of launching her debut EP.

For a fifteen-year-old, Billie had secured a degree of creative control unprecedented in the music industry. She had come up with the title, *dont smile at me*; the sometimes-unconventional song titles; the track listing and order (which were decided upon in a series of texts to Finneas in the early hours of the morning); and the cover image for the EP. She had gone to the label asking to pose with a red stepladder against a yellow background while dressed in all in red "with a million chains." Miraculously, the label had agreed. Variations of the stunning image with Billie hanging from the top of the ladder or sitting sulkily underneath would accompany interviews and tour promotions and even Billie's own merchandise over the next six months.

The title gave Billie a concept on which to hang her image. She was, and intended to be, nobody's plaything. It was a provocative and assertive title and one that she was more than happy to riff upon. Those who had followed Billie over the last year had, of course, seen her smile in photographs and in interviews. She had a great sense of humor and clearly liked to laugh, but here she was reacting to the pressure she felt to smile (and to make music that wasn't sad and depressing) when perhaps she didn't feel like it. "I hate smiling," she said on numerous occasions. "It makes me feel weak and powerless and small." She said how she resented having to smile back at people who smile at her in the street and, for the first time, claimed to have "a resting bitch face" that looked sad all of the time.

She was, and intended to be, nobody's plaything.

However, she seemed pretty happy at the launch party for the EP at—where else?—the Hi Hat, her local club. Friends and fans dressed in either red or yellow (later, during "COPYCAT," Billie tried to separate them and make them mimic one another's dancing); and there was free candy and a photo booth where they could pose on the now-iconic red ladder.

Billie, in a padded orange gilet, and Finneas, looking supercool in a T-shirt reading "Too young to go to jail" around the collar (he was still only twenty!), proceeded to play the short set of tracks from the EP. The packed audience lapped it up, and Billie was in her element, even naming the subject of "my boy," Henry, who was there in the crowd.

Dont smile at me was released on August 11, 2017. It contained eight tracks: the recent run of four singles along with "ocean eyes," "bellyache," and two previously unrecorded tracks that had formed part of her live set list. The first of these was "party favor"—a real live favorite. In contrast to the brooding, synth-dominated sound of the rest of the EP, this is a happy singsong with Billie playing ukulele to a clickety-clack backbeat. All this saccharine sweetness is naturally undercut by the ruthless Billie dumping her beau on his birthday in a voice message. You can call back, she suggests, but I'll have probably blocked you by then. Savage or what? The other new track, "hostage," a love song, completes the EP. Billie sings the ballad-style track in a calm, tender voice, and although there is no vicious side, there is still a dark undercurrent, from the refrain about crawling inside the boy's veins to the whole hostage metaphor of restraining someone against their will. If we didn't know already that Billie couldn't—or wouldn't—write an ordinary song, we did now.

And so an era that had begun with a bedroom-composed song on SoundCloud came to an end over eighteen months later with eight bedroom-composed songs on an album released by an international record company. The songs on the EP varied in style and subject, but were distinctive and recognizable as Billie Eilish songs. They often touched upon dark aspects and, although

> **You can call back, she suggests, but I'll have probably blocked you by then.**

While a few used the "gloom pop" tag to criticize the tracks as too downbeat, many more noted the diversity both in lyrics and in style.

mature in composition, didn't try to hide a teenage sentimentality. Billie admitted, partly in jest, that she never wrote songs about how much she loved someone—only songs that said "I hate you" or "You make me hate me." It would be another twelve months before Billie's profile rose high enough to land *dont smile at me* a chart position, but for now there was a strong and growing base following, not only in the US but in the UK, Canada, New Zealand, and Australia.

Those reviewing the EP were unanimous in their appreciation of the witty, crafted lyrics, of Billie's vocal range and adaptability, and her effortless harmonizing with Finneas. While a few used the "gloom pop" tag to criticize the tracks as too downbeat, many more noted the diversity both in lyrics and in style. Overwhelmingly, the reaction was one of awe at the talent displayed by a fifteen-year-old songwriter and performer. They saw in Billie a raw talent that was only going to get better.

CHAPTER SIX
ON THE ROAD

When is a star not a star? Back in August 2017, Billie Eilish didn't consider herself a star.

She was a pretty grounded, normal teenager with best friends, crushes, mood swings, and a love of TV and music, especially music—any conversation would be littered with references to popular and obscure artists. She had a whole bunch of opinions and wasn't afraid to give them, and treated any "fans" like personal friends, engaging with them on Snapchat, Instagram, Twitter, or Facebook. It's a state of affairs she would have been happy to continue, but Billie also loved to perform and wanted her songs to be heard by as many people as possible. After the release of the EP, it was clear she would be a star and her life would change—but, amid the glamor, lights, and screaming crowds, the old Highland Park Billie would never be hard to spot . . .

That month, as the EP made her more and more fans, Billie livestreamed from the house on Instagram. Unrehearsed and beautifully raw, she sang accompanied only by her own guitar, ukulele, or piano. She played covers of a number of songs, including "The Hill" originally recorded by Czech singer-songwriter Markéta Irglová, "Jealous" by British singer Labrinth, and "Dancing on My Own" by the Swedish artist Robyn. She even sang in Spanish with a version of the 1970s worldwide hit "Eres Tú." These performances showed Billie's ability to not only interpret other artists' songs but also to own them with an emotionally charged vocal.

In the comfort of her home, we were able to see the unguarded Billie. In one long and rambling livestream, she just answered fans' questions as they came through and talked a little about her life. She was so open, talking about boys and her relationships, recognizing names of friends who sent messages, and marveling at how she had such support from as far afield as Brazil and Mexico. Sometimes, however, the black clouds that she later said would descend in her life in this period became apparent and the "I'm so sad" she utters at the end of one stream is completely heartbreaking.

The livestream also included her previously unheard songs that she had written. One, which featured her singing to a ukulele, fans would call "see-through." A beautiful ballad of the difficulties and pain experienced in a broken relationship, it would finally appear two years later in its studio version as the song "8" on the *When We All Fall Asleep, Where Do We Go?* album. At that point, Billie explained that the song was written from the perspective of someone she had hurt rather than from personal heartbreak.

Another livestream song, which came to be known as "limbo" or "7 DAYS," has still to be recorded, but that hasn't stopped fans uploading self-made videos

These performances showed Billie's ability to not only interpret other artists' songs but also to own them with an emotionally charged vocal.

for the track to YouTube or cover versions to SoundCloud. It features Billie at the piano with the most delicate of vocals. Telling the story of a relationship that has run its course with the lyric, "We're broken glass waiting to be washed away," Billie plucks at the heartstrings. Why it has never been released remains a mystery, and fans live in hope that a studio version will one day appear.

To Billie's apparent amazement, the sellout shows in Auckland in New Zealand, and Sydney and Melbourne in Australia, saw fans singing every lyric—even to "limbo."

"Limbo" was initially on the set list for Billie's short visit to the Southern Hemisphere soon after the release of the EP. Fans from Australia and New Zealand had been among the most enthusiastic of her initial overseas devotees, and they were rewarded with the full set of songs from *dont smile at me*. To Billie's apparent amazement, the sellout shows in Auckland in New Zealand, and Sydney and Melbourne in Australia, saw fans singing every lyric—even to "limbo." Finneas was now getting his own moment in the spotlight. Midshow, Billie walked to the side of the stage and announced her brother was going to sing a song. It was her idea, and she knew her fans would be receptive. Finneas sang his own single "I'm in Love without You," and of course, the audience loved it.

There was one more new treat added to the set list for the tour Down Under. Early in the shows, as Billie picked up her ukulele, the crowd cheered in expectation of "party favor." Instead, she headed straight into a pared-down version of "Hotline Bling," replacing Drake's low burr with her sometimes rasping and sometimes sweet-as-pie falsetto (when the audience sing-alongs inevitably began, many had trouble with those high notes!). It would soon become a live favorite.

Billie's performances were improving with every show. She'd managed to transfer her true character to her stage persona with all the energy, the don't-give-a-damn attitude, the passion for her music, and the love of the fans on display. It wasn't an act; it was for real. The audiences recognized she was being herself, whether she was singing, dancing, or chatting between songs. "I just try to be as hype as I can on stage and have a lot of fun," she told the *NZ Herald*. "My goal is to get people moshing in the crowd one day. My music isn't there yet and people aren't there yet, but I love moshing . . . I don't want anybody to not move in the crowd."

It was her slickest and biggest-budget video yet. Although directed by Megan Park, much of it derives from Billie's imagination.

Back in the US, Billie had two weeks to wait until setting off on her North American tour. It would be a period in which her profile soared higher and higher. Within days a new video had dropped for "watch." It was her slickest and biggest-budget video yet. Although directed by Megan Park, much of it derives from Billie's imagination. In a dark space, a group of women (dressed in baggy, colorful sportswear as if they had plundered Billie's wardrobe) lie on four orange Dodge Challengers (Billie's favorite car and color). When Billie enters and climbs the now-familiar red stepladder in the center of the space, the music stops, and in an uncomfortable silence the women tie Billie to the ladder and pour fuel around the base.

Billie's vision ended there. She explained that it was too short, and Megan Park added the interspersed scenes of Billie dressed in comfy white clothes in a bedroom. This symbolized the new Billie, now free of her hurt and heartbroken self. Intense, thought-provoking, and visually stunning, the video was another creative expression from an artist who was continuing to surprise everyone.

Fans were still digesting this when Apple announced Billie as its latest Up Next artist. The Up Next campaign aimed to support rising acts by using "all of its resources to give their music visibility to new audiences." Billie was following in the footsteps of her friend Khalid, the previous Up Next pick, who had profited greatly from the spotlight. Up Next meant a glossily shot documentary that combined archive footage from her childhood and comments from her parents with footage of her and Finneas rehearsing at home, and an interview with Billie. Alongside it the pair released three live tracks—"bellyache," "watch," and "ocean eyes"—with videos of the performance fabulously shot in high definition in a room looking out on to the LA night skyline.

Perhaps the best thing about being an Apple Up Next artist was that Billie got to sing on *The Late Late Show with James Corden*. Introduced by Zane Lowe, she confidently strode out, dressed in a yellow turtleneck sweater, oversized jacket, and pants with her silver hair tied back. Finneas hung back in the shadows playing keyboards as she delivered "ocean eyes" sitting and kneeling on a yellow-framed light box. It was an assured performance that went out to a million viewers.

She confidently strode out, dressed in a yellow turtleneck sweater, oversized jacket, and pants with her silver hair tied back.

The stage was set for Billie's first-ever headline tour, involving a string of dates across the country and into Canada. Every concert had sold out—back in the spring when the shows were being arranged, Billie and her team just hadn't anticipated the reach she would have by that fall. With more and more fans getting on board every day, the 200- to 400-capacity venues they had booked were now just not big enough. Even the biggest of them, the 500-capacity Crocodile in Seattle, sold out in less than half an hour.

Going on the road for a month or more was a completely different affair from playing a couple of dates on successive nights. Firstly, she needed a support act and, naturally, Billie already had someone in mind. Thutmose, a fellow LA resident, was beginning to make a name for himself. The Nigerian-born, Brooklyn-raised rapper's video of himself freestyling Kendrick Lamar's "Humble" earned a million views in a week—and the attention of Billie, who was looking for someone to set the mood for her concerts. She needed a tour manager, too, and

With more and more fans getting on board every day, the 200- to 400-capacity venues they had booked were now just not big enough.

was fixed up with Brian Marquis, who had been touring with punk and hardcore bands since the turn of the century. Brian's knowledge of the dives and back-room venues up and down the country was invaluable, but he would remain a vital part of Billie's team as she graduated to concert halls and arenas.

She also needed road crew to drive the van, help set up, and operate the lights. Enter Patrick O'Connell, Billie's dad. Having had limited opportunities to act, he had taken a job using his woodworking skills to build sets for Barbie dolls, but with the rest of the family taking to the road—Maggie would chaperone the still underage Billie—he wasn't going to be left behind. He just needed to master the lighting, and he was the ideal one-man crew. "I thought, 'When is this ever gonna happen again?'" he told *Rolling Stone*. "I wanted to be a part of it, because it's pretty darn cool." And so they packed the outfits, instruments, and T-shirts for the merch stall and, like one of their old family holidays, all climbed into a small van. They stuck to cheap hotels and the whole family would often have to share a single room, but, hey, it was all part of the adventure.

The tour played eleven shows in seventeen days, beginning in LA; traveling up the West Coast to Seattle via Oregon; heading cross-country to Chicago, into Canada for a show in Toronto, back down the East Coast to New York, Cambridge (Massachusetts), and Philadelphia; and finishing in Washington, DC. The traveling must have been exhausting, let alone getting up onstage most nights and having to perform.

Billie was now officially on the radar (certainly if a mention on Kim Kardashian's Snapchat is the measure), and fans would be lining up at the doors and filling the venues hours before she was due onstage. The intimate venues were packed with teens, music-savvy twentysomethings, and a smattering of parents lingering at the back. It was great for Thutmose, who had a packed house to play for, and they were well and truly hyped by the time Billie bounded on to the stage after a few bars of the theme from her favorite TV comedy, *The Office*.

The set would open with "COPYCAT," a track that immediately got fans moving (they loved the "Psych!" moment, when Billie gave the finger and everyone went wild). Then, for an hour, she held the audience spellbound. While Finneas stood

The traveling must have been exhausting, never mind getting up onstage most nights and having to perform.

Billie has broken records as a female artist, including being the first female artist to win all the "big four" GRAMMYs.

by his keyboard, Billie used the whole area, prowling the stage edge to get as close to fans as possible, bouncing up and down, flicking her hair, holding the mic for the audience to sing, cheesily dancing next to Finneas, or standing at the mic stand swaying with her whole body. The audience was sucked in by the ebb and flow of the set list, as Billie built the energy, took it down with a slower number, and gradually raised it again. She finished the set with "ocean eyes"—one song everyone in the crowd knew—before returning for an encore with a rousing anthemic version of "bellyache." As good as these tracks sounded in the studio, the live performance, feeding off the fans' energy and passion, took them to another level—and the audience knew it. Billie wouldn't be playing venues this small for much longer.

The unreleased "limbo" was replaced in the set list for the tour by another as-yet-unrecorded song called "listen before i go," which had been played for the first time at the Melbourne concert. There is a beauty in its simplicity as its straight verse-and-chorus structure is softly played out to a piano accompaniment, but this is a suicide note in song: poignant and desolate, full of despair and self-recrimination, and tainted with bitterness. It is difficult to listen to with the knowledge that Billie was experiencing real depression around this time. In a year or so, at a concert in Toronto, when it was still to be recorded, she would explain that she didn't want the song to bring fans down but to act as a "mental hug," sharing emotions to make them bearable.

One more new song was debuted on October 21 in Philadelphia for the encore of the penultimate show of the tour. It was one that dedicated fans would have heard on a livestream just a few days before the tour had begun, when Billie had sung a particularly downbeat (as her mood dictated) version of "wish you were gay," accompanying herself on the guitar. Even at that point she was aware of the way the song might be read, saying, "That's so not meant to be offensive in any way. It literally means I wish he was gay so that he didn't like me for an actual reason."

WOMEN'S RIGHTS

Billie has never proclaimed herself a feminist, but everything she has said and done would suggest that women's rights are at the very core of her beliefs. Though her upbringing and forthright confident personality have ensured that nothing will prevent her from doing what she wants, Billie also understands that the right for women to have their voices heard, to be able to dress how they please, and even to be seen as cool and interesting were hard fought for in the pop world.

Billie has broken records as a female artist, including being the first female artist to win all the "big four" GRAMMYs and the only female artist to land fourteen songs on the *Billboard* Top 100 in a single week. In her *Billboard* Woman of the Year speech in December 2019, she thanked the women in the music industry who had "paved the way" for her success. Talking of Ariana Grande, Taylor Swift, and others, she recognized that "women who, in the past, have done what they weren't supposed to do, has made my life a lot easier and made me able to do what I want and be who I want." She wants to be that kind of groundbreaker herself and has said how thrilled she is to be in the wave of new female artists (she mentions Princess Nokia, Jessie Reyez, and Kodie Shane) who get girls jumping and moshing at concerts, something that was once the domain of male acts.

Billie has made it abundantly clear that she doesn't want to tell her supporters or anyone else what to think or do. This, of course, does not mean she always keeps her own views private. In 2019 she took to Instagram to say that she loves to go to Atlanta, Georgia, and play shows there, but objected to their lawmakers' decision to take away women's rights after the state clamped down on women's access to abortion. She also joined Lady Gaga, Ariana Grande, and other musicians in supporting the Planned Parenthood Federation's campaign for reproductive rights.

Some point to Billie's signature baggy clothes as being a rejection of sexualization of women in pop music. The reason for Billie's style, however, is complicated and not necessarily a statement. It is bound up with her own fashion sense, her mental and physical comfort, and a desire to keep some of herself secret from the world. There is no doubt that in wearing loose-fitting, sometimes oversized clothes, Billie is refusing to conform to the media's image of women singers, but she refuses to condemn those who do and has reserved the right to wear more revealing clothes if she should wish.

Billie was emerging as an incredible talent, as Europe now witnessed. The sellout tour went to Paris, Amsterdam, Stockholm, and Berlin, and saw a return to London.

Billie was creating a real bond with fans—she was one of them, and they recognized it.

Everywhere she went the small venues were packed, and she created a buzz that remained long after she'd gone. Billie was creating a real bond with fans—she was one of them, and they recognized it. At those intimate concerts, she could pick out every face, grasp every outstretched hand, meet with anyone who hung behind afterward, and even post Instagram mini-movies of them at the show. She wasn't acting the star and had no intention of being one, but when it comes, it comes. And it was coming . . .

ON THE ROAD

CHAPTER SEVEN
THE ONE TO WATCH

Stop telling everyone you're gonna make it, just mind ya business and go make it.

Billie had tweeted this during the tour, and she was certainly practicing what she preached and working like crazy. She was playing live, performing for YouTube channels, and even trying out her skills at live entertainment.

In October 2017 she and Finneas had performed acoustic versions of "COPYCAT" and "party favor" for the Mahogany Sessions YouTube channel. Against a deserted industrial setting, Billie, wearing an eye-catching spiked choker, gave an exquisite vocal and dramatic performance to just a guitar or ukulele accompaniment. This stripped-back version showed how authentic and beautiful her voice was. Then, while on tour in New York, she had appeared on MTV's revived live show *TRL*, helping an audience member win $250 on "Older or Younger" (example question: "Is Billie older or younger than an iPhone?"), answering rapid-fire questions from DJ Khaled, and giving another different but still bewitching performance of "ocean eyes."

All this had ensured the EP continued to be picked up by

fans and the media with *dont smile at me* even breaking the US *Billboard* 200 Chart, reaching Number 185 in early November. Billie then issued a surprise release. She dropped a new track, named "bitches broken hearts," that was available only on SoundCloud. This was a result of a collaboration with Emmit Fenn that had taken place a year before. Fenn's track "Painting Greys" had been a viral hit around the same time as "ocean eyes" and Billie, taken by his captivating and idiosyncratic electronica sound, had wanted to work with him. On Facebook, Fenn explained, "The song was finished in a couple hours, no post production was done, no mixing, no mastering, we just thought it was perfect how it was."

A moody synth backing and a beat intriguingly echoed by a deep male voice and snippets of crowd noise.

"Bitches broken hearts" is a goose-bump-inducing diatribe against an ex who hid his true feelings and paid the price by losing her. Against a moody synth backing and a beat intriguingly echoed by a deep male voice and snippets of crowd noise, Billie's straight but incredibly powerful delivery summing up the aftermath of an emotional impasse cuts to the quick. Her soft, matter-of-fact vocals are magnificently undercut not only by the title line but also by the tragic penultimate line of "I guess being lonely fits me." The track amassed more than six hundred thousand streams in its first week on SoundCloud and was enthusiastically received. *Nylon* magazine praised it as a "hypnotic ode to the bittersweetness of lost love and fresh starts," while the influential music blog *Pigeons & Planes* extolled the track's "woozy blend of electric piano, vocal samples and sparse percussion."

It was the perfect time to announce the next tour. Titled the Wheres My Mind Tour, with reference to the line in "bellyache," it was even more ambitious than the one they had just finished. Beginning in February, it scheduled in concerts in eight countries in Europe and seventeen shows across North America. Tickets for the tour sold out in less than an hour.

At the end of each year, the media like to predict who next year's breakthrough artists will be, and in 2017 the name Billie Eilish was on many lips. Vevo were the first to name-drop her, putting her first on their "DSCVR Artists to Watch 2018" list. Billie and Finneas gave a live performance of "my boy" for them, and it was special. Billie's vocals are so smooth, and she dances across the sparse room injecting so much energy into the song. Even Finneas joins in a brief synchronized dance. In the UK, the BBC also named her in its celebrated Sound of 2018 list, voted for by critics, broadcasters, DJs, and other music-industry figures. She was the youngest-ever nominee for the title but didn't land a place in its top five, with Norwegian singer Sigrid eventually topping the poll.

Lots of other magazines, blogs, and radio shows were quick to pick Billie as their one to watch for 2018, but for many she was already a favorite. New Zealand and neighboring Australia had been among the first countries to take her to their heart, and this was confirmed in December, when Billie appeared on the cover of New Zealand's pop culture magazine *Coup De Main*. It was her first-ever magazine cover, and the photo was stunning. Wearing a bright yellow top, she was framed against a black background, her head tilted slightly to the left, her silver hair partially plaited at the front, with a gold chain and earrings (one a giant hoop), her pale lips forming that neutral nonsmile, and underneath the pronounced eyebrows a stare that pierces right through you, each eye accentuated by a thick red line running around it like a mask.

But before the year end, Billie had one more treat in store for new and old fans. On December 14, the track "&burn" appeared. Essentially a reworking of "watch," it had one added ingredient:

Vince Staples. For her first vocal collaboration, Billie had picked the hip-hop artist whose 2017 album *Big Fish Theory* had been a hit around the world over the summer. Billie had long been a fan of his innovative, boundary-pushing approach to rap, and Staples was her first choice when she considered who could feature on "&burn."

"Watch" was originally going to be called "watch & burn" (a play on "watch and learn"), but when two very different versions emerged in the studio, the title was split between the two. "&burn" is an altogether moodier affair, with less piano and a production that plays with intriguing effects and Billie's voice (including the addition of an extra syllable to "start-ted"). Billie and Finneas immediately felt it was perfect for a rap-break verse, and Staples's rapid-fire, understated delivery fits effortlessly into the track. His contribution feels natural rather than a wedged-in guest appearance, and adds energy and variety to the pared-back version.

The track also added to Billie's growing catalogue of diverse and addictive recordings. She remained a left-field artist, so though her tracks were all accumulating serious streaming and downloading numbers, they were still not big enough to earn her

Among all this music-business talk it is easy to forget that she was still a child.

a spot on the charts. Among all this music-business talk, it is easy to forget that she was still a child. On December 18, 2017, Billie celebrated her sixteenth birthday. In the *Coup De Main* interview a month earlier she had said she had always wanted a sweet sixteen party, but now wasn't sure. "I'm kind of in a transitional period with friends," she told them. "So there's not really anyone I feel that cares enough about me to be with me on my birthday." Many find teenage friendship issues a problem, and for Billie, suddenly thrown into an adult world and spending so much time away from home, it was extra difficult.

We now know that for a lengthy period Billie had been suffering from depression. This was not just a matter of mood swings, but issues of anxiety, body image, insecurity, and irrational sadness that affects so many teenagers. Billie first revealed her problems with depression in an interview with *Rolling Stone* magazine in July 2019, just a few months after she felt her own dark clouds had finally left her.

She credited the care of her mother, her love of playing the shows, and the chance to meet fans with helping her get through the hardest times.

In this and in subsequent interviews she told how the injury that had prevented her from dancing had sent her into a downward spiral. This coincided with the original success of "ocean eyes" and continued through her seventeenth year—the blossoming of stardom that seemed so thrilling to the outsider. "I was so unhappy and joyless," Billie told US TV host Gayle King in 2020, confessing, "I didn't ever think I would be happy again, ever." She credited the care of her mother, her love of playing the shows, and the chance to meet fans with helping her get through the hardest times. There were plenty of people who followed Billie on Twitter or watched her livestreams through this period who had an idea of what she was going through, but most, those who just watched her performances on YouTube or listened to the tracks, had little idea how she was feeling. At least now, with hindsight, we can review the events of 2018—the year in which it hit her hardest—in the context of her struggle with severe depression.

"Idontwannabeyouanymore," Billie's most obvious depression song, had, with the exception of "ocean eyes," proved to be the most popular of her tracks so far, and early in the new year it was given an official video release. Shot in a 16:9 ratio, so it can be best viewed on a cell phone, the video is set in a totally white room. Billie, dressed in an all-white, oversized hooded jumpsuit, sings while staring herself down in a mirror. That's it. But she manages to fill it with drama and sad beauty. Meanwhile, proof of the enduring popularity of "ocean eyes" came in late January when the track received an official Gold certification from the Recording Industry Association of America (RIAA). The certification recognizes five hundred thousand units, with each unit representing one paid download or 150 streams.

Billie's first engagements of 2018 came a long way from home. She was booked as one of the artists on the Laneway Festival. Featuring a number of indie-styled acts playing a series of festivals across Australia and New Zealand, Laneway has become one of the highlights of the summer Down Under. The festival also introduced Billie to a new continent, as the first event took place in Singapore.

ANDREW MARSHALL

Before heading out on tour, Billie and Finneas decided to enlist a drummer to add energy and drama to their live show. After some auditions they found Andrew Marshall. Nearer to Finneas's age than Billie's, New Yorker Andrew had previously played with a number of bands—usually at the same time. They included pop rock duo Ex Cops, indie band Tigertown, and songwriting duo Marian Hill (who had remixed

"bellyache"). What was key for Billie and Finneas was that, like them, Andrew liked to work across genres—from pop and trap to electronica and hip-hop—and that he was a modern drummer at ease with conventional and electronic drums, and playing a mixture of the two in what is called a hybrid kit.

Before stepping out onstage, Andrew has to adapt the sounds Finneas creates electronically into the live sound they are looking for. He is responsible not only for the beats but for playing any sampled sounds, such as doors slamming or glass breaking, at exactly the right moment. Sometimes they want to replicate the recorded sound of a song, and other times they deliberately alter it—perhaps giving it an acoustic feel or creating a dance vibe. His job is to work out and execute a live drum sound that fits their objectives and, at the same time, brings some real energy to the party.

Andrew's debut with Billie and Finneas came in Singapore in 2017, and he stayed for the whole Wheres My Mind Tour. Despite being the outsider, he fit into the family setup that is Billie on tour and remained an integral, if unsung, member of the team as they progressed from playing three-hundred-capacity clubs to the world's biggest festivals.

Billie shouted to the fans in Singapore that it was the first festival she'd played where anyone had turned out to see her. She took to the stage in a sports short suit—a baggy short-sleeved shirt and shorts that extend below the knee. It was a look beloved of rappers from Pharrell to A$AP and one we would soon get used to seeing Billie wear. This particular outfit was gold and black and bore the logo Damani Dada, a 1990s brand favored by hip-hop artists. It was also the same retro outfit Drake had attracted interest with when he wore it in his 2013 video for "No New Friends."

Like nearly all of Billie's shows, the Laneway concerts were restricted to ages eighteen and up (in the US many venues were even ages twenty-one and up). Often Billie herself, as a sixteen-year-old, would be confined to the backstage area. However, during the Laneway series, her booking agents did manage to squeeze in one all-ages show back at the Tuning Fork in Auckland, and Billie and Finneas both had something special in store for the young audience.

First, Finneas appeared midway through the set with a new song, "New Girl," a preview of his single, which was to be released the following week. Then, after "party favor," Billie moved to the front of the stage, sat down, and made the crowd back up. Face-to-face with an audience (and their phones) largely of her own age, she sang "when the party's over"—the first time it had ever been performed to anyone apart from her managers. As she started singing to Finneas's soft piano accompaniment, a hush came over the crowd. It was a real shared moment for Billie and the fans in what she described as one of the most fun shows she'd ever had.

"When the party's over" portrays a relationship breaking down.

"When the party's over" portrays a relationship breaking down. Finneas had written it on his own in the autumn and had come up with the title to link it to "party favor." Billie talked about how excited he was when he called her into his room so she could hear it. She had work to do, too, though, because the vocal line spanned several octaves and really tested the strength of her voice. Having rehearsed it, they decided to introduce it into the set soon—it was just a matter of choosing the right moment. Maybe considered too intimate for the festival crowd, the song wasn't played at any of the other Laneway shows, but after Auckland

As she started singing to Finneas's soft piano accompaniment, a hush came over the crowd.

it took its place in the set list for the small venues—and remained a favorite.

The Laneway trip came to a close at the beginning of February, but before they left, Billie and Finneas had a parting gift for their fans Down Under (and everyone else thanks to YouTube). They appeared on Australian national alternative-music station Triple J to take part in their Like a Version session, where artists play a song of their own as well as a song by someone else that they love. They gave an acoustic performance of "bellyache," once again astounding listeners with their ability to create different and spellbinding versions of their own songs. But they also showed they could do it with others' compositions too. Their take on Michael Jackson's "Bad" was the first cover we had heard Billie sing outside of the livestreams, and it was remarkable. She managed to own one of the most popular hits ever by turning it into a Billie Eilish song—slow, mellow, and real.

It was only six weeks into 2018, and already Billie had played concerts and launched what was to be one of her biggest songs. But it wasn't about to slow down; she still had three more months of solid touring to do.

CHAPTER EIGHT
LOVELY

On Valentine's Day 2018, Billie was onstage at the famous Heaven club in London.

Appropriately she had a romantic tale to relay. She told of how she'd had a date two years earlier on the eve of Valentine's Day. She and a boy had been to see a lousy film and then gone to the roof to sit and watch the stars. That's when it happened, she told an audience who were hanging on to her every word: her first kiss. But this was Billie, so it didn't end there. With evident disgust she revealed that the boy told her that it wasn't as "magical" as he thought it would be—and with that the opening chords of "my boy" struck up.

That story was repeated as the tour wound its way through Paris, Milan, Stockholm, Amsterdam, Brussels, Berlin, Cologne, and Oslo, before she landed back in LA. She could have had nearly a week off then, but she couldn't resist a festival and the Okeechobee Music & Arts Festival in Florida was calling. In no time she was setting off on tour again. The sold-out tour began with a show in her home city and then moved on to the iconic Great American Music Hall in San Francisco. It was here that a fan took a film of the "first kiss" story. When she uploaded it to YouTube a year later, it had an additional punch line, because in this version she went on to dedicate "my boy" to Henry—even sharing his last name. Remember poor Henry? Having been humiliated in front of his friends in LA, he now faced the ire of hundreds of Billie's fans who tracked him down on social media to harass him for his treatment of their idol.

The 2018 North American Wheres My Mind Tour poster featured Billie dressed in layers of green and standing awkwardly on billowy green fabric. It listed more cities and bigger venues (this time they visited seven-hundred-capacity bars, clubs, and halls) than the Dont Smile at Me Tour, but all still sold out within an hour. Billie's team had also upped their game to ensure the show was engaging and dynamic. Andrew Marshall was now employed as Billie's regular live drummer, and they invested in an automated lighting system—a white screen framed by bulbs—that synchronized with the sound-mixing software.

Although the opener was still an emerging act, alt-hip-hop artist Reo Cragun was known to some of the audiences as he had recently released a successful album called *Growing Pains*. His positivity and banter with tour DJ Keiro would bring the crowd to boiling point before two (toy) gun-toting men dressed in white overalls and wearing green Billie Eilish bandanas as face masks burst on to the stage. When they shot at the audience, the guns showered the expectant crowd with billion-dollar bills that featured Billie's face.

The guns showered the expectant crowd with billion-dollar bills that featured Billie's face.

As the men (who the audience now realized were Finneas and Andrew) took their place behind the keyboard and drums, the stage was set for Billie's entrance.

For this tour Billie opted for darker gray hair and wore her hip-hop-inspired clothes—often a hoodie, beanie, and gold chains—or oversized patterned suits. In the live shows she had become a force of nature. She would jump and feverishly bop across the stage, involve Finneas in dance moves, or hog the front of the stage, crouching to look eye to eye at the audience. Toward the end of the show, she would try to get the mosh pit going or even jump down into the crowd (after they'd promised to dance with her and not crush her). In the ballads she would stand still at the mic, but kept the audience's gaze fixed on her as she gracefully swayed and danced with her arms and hands.

> **Toward the end of the show, she would try to get the mosh pit going or even jump down into the crowd.**

Most noticeable of all was how she maintained the bond with her fans. She would repeatedly tell them how much they meant to her, she would reach out and grab the outstretched hands, and when she spoke, there was none of the bullish, don't-care-what-you-think attitude reserved for the general public—she was a sweet and self-deprecating teenager who was among friends. Perhaps the most powerful moment came when she sang "when the party's over" and she would ask them, even if they were filming on their phones, to engage with her directly, to share the moment and cement a bond between them.

Those who witnessed a live performance from Billie in these times were privileged indeed. Never again would she play to such an intimate crowd and be able to interact directly with her fans. When each show finished, she would go back to the dressing room, have a bottle of water, and then go out to talk to those who stayed to meet her. At some shows she stayed for three to four hours to make sure she had met everyone.

The tour was divided in March by a five-day return to the SXSW Festival in Austin. The year before, Billie had played to curious audiences who knew little about her. This year she played in five different venues. Perhaps best of all were a return to the Central Presbyterian Church at SXSW, where she and Finneas played a special acoustic midnight show, and being pretty unanimously picked as the breakout artist of the festival. What a difference a year made!

Those who couldn't get tickets for the concerts were given a taste of what they were missing when the tour hit New York, and Billie appeared on the super-popular *Tonight Show Starring Jimmy Fallon*. In a set drenched with yellow light and punctuated with white strobes, Billie took the stage in the brown Gucci Imran Potato short suit (complete with matching socks!) that she sported on the tour with Andrew and Finneas in their stage costumes of white overalls and bandana face masks. It was a scintillating performance as Billie danced, leaped, staggered, and pouted around the stage, even kneeling at the front to sing to her TV-watching fans.

To some it might have been confusing to see this young woman dressed like a rapper, strutting around like a rock-and-roll star, and singing like a diva, but to those who got it, this was the real Billie. But so was the Billie who performed in the show's Cover Room (where artists record their favorite songs for the show's website). Billie's intense bossa-nova acoustic rendition—with fabulous harmonizing by Finneas—of the Strokes's track "Call Me Back" serving as more proof of their ability to interpret others' songs and add something special.

The tour came to an end in April and was celebrated with a short souvenir video from photographer and videographer Gibson Hazard. If *The Tonight Show* was an indication of Billie's popular appeal, then a Gibson Hazard tour video gave her a certain hip-hop credibility. The twenty-two-year-old Hazard had earned a reputation for groundbreaking editing techniques in his work on surreal tour videos for rap artists including Drake, Wiz Khalifa, and Future. His *Wheres My Mind Tour* video was no exception. Looking like a multimillion-dollar movie trailer it combined concert footage, 3D effects, and CGI to a broken mash-up soundtrack of her songs. It featured Billie standing among falling billion-dollar bills, leaping from a burning skyscraper, flying horror-movie-style through a cemetery, and jumping onstage in front of ecstatic fans. It really made you wish there was a full movie on the way.

BILLIE THE VEGAN

In 2019 Billie took to Instagram to help celebrate the tenth anniversary of the international campaign Meat Free Mondays. "I've been vegetarian my whole life, vegan for five years," she wrote. "Help the world—I try." Billie has never known what it is like to eat meat and has no desire to do so (although she once confessed to accidentally swallowing an ant that was swimming in her soy milk). At the age of twelve she made her own decision to become vegan and remains so to this day.

Billie herself rarely mentions the issue, although interviewers occasionally feel it merits raising. She has said that she is vegan for a number of reasons, but mainly that she loves animals. "I just think there's no point in creating something out of an animal when the animal is already there," was her logic when questioned on Tumblr, signing off with, "Leave animals alone." A rare occasion of Billie getting vocal on animal-welfare issues

came in June 2019, when she shared video footage of workers physically abusing newborn calves on a farm in Indiana. She commented that if anyone can watch that and not care that they are contributing to the cruelty, then she pities them.

None of this should imply that Billie doesn't like her food. Her mouth waters at the thought of her mom's mashed potatoes and gravy, she loves her avocados (when she can find them), her coffee preference is for a Starbucks salted caramel Frappuccino (with soy milk and extra caramel), and she loves to bake peanut-butter cookies when she gets time in her own kitchen. Most of all, though, she adores burritos—"I'm going to get 18 bean burritos with only beans," she said at a Taco Bell drive-through window in a 2019 Instagram video (they were for a party!).

She has said that being vegan was difficult when touring in the early days as they were on a budget and vegan food could be hard to find, especially in Europe. Nowadays, of course, she is well catered to wherever she goes and even made a vegan road trip for an Uber Eats promotion that listed her favorite vegan restaurants across the US. The menu ranged from Electrified Wild Blueberry Pancakes in Austin to a Love Life Salad ("one of the most Instagrammable meals in the land") in Miami to Guac Burgers with cashew-cheese sauce and shiitake bacon in New York. And her advice when you can't get good vegan food? Just eat some chips.

"Bitches broken hearts" had been released as a single during the tour, but there seemed no sign of any brand-new material being released. Then, on April 19, 2018, just two weeks after the tour came to a close, Billie tweeted, "Lovely with @thegreatkhalid." That was the modest fanfare for the appearance of "lovely," a duet between Billie and rising star Khalid. Incredibly, the track was not some contrived mash-up of fresh, new talent, but the result of friends getting together and writing a song.

The two artists had much in common. Khalid had broken through with "Location," an electronic R & B track with hip-hop influence, which had been a viral hit around the same time as Billie's "ocean eyes." A friend had played the song to her, but at the time it wasn't available on any mainstream store (it would eventually reach Number 17 in the Hot 100). Finally, she tracked it down on SoundCloud and was amazed to discover that Khalid was already following her on Twitter. She got in touch, and the two young artists hit it off, meeting up when Khalid attended one of her first shows in LA back in 2016. Khalid admired the fact that Billie wasn't a typical teenager. Her carefree attitude appealed to him: she wore what she wanted and said exactly what she felt. At the time neither of them knew their music would be successful, but they recognized the talent and star quality in each other.

The friends hadn't planned to record together. "He just came over and we hung out. Me and my brother hung out with Khalid in our house," Billie told Zane Lowe on his Beats 1 radio show. "And it was literally, this is us hanging out as friends and we ended up writing a song." Sitting in Finneas's bedroom, they had been playing around with ideas just for fun, and Billie had come up with a melody. As they repeated and repeated it, it dawned on the three of them that they had to do something with it.

Together, they pieced together lyrics that meant something to them: a song about trying and failing to escape depression. This was a feeling that Billie was experiencing all too frequently around this period, but it was also an issue with which Khalid was familiar. Back in December he had even tweeted, "I'm not feeling the best RN and my anxiety is super bad." The song was a devastating description of a fragile, painful, and frustrated frame of mind laced with the sarcasm of "Isn't it lovely" and "Welcome home."

Finneas was left to work his magic on the track. Over the following months, he had built upon the vocal and piano track they had made that day. He layered the voices and introduced a soft percussion, but essentially he gave the track a swirling, heart-wrenching vibe by the introduction of a violin. This was played by Madison Leinster, who had become a YouTube star with her violin covers of pop hits. "You can't fake strings like that," Finneas would write of the virtuoso on Instagram.

This was another big step for Billie. It was a real duet, not just the inserted verse that Vince Staples had supplied for "&burn." Khalid was a star on the rise with a bigger profile than her's; he already had three Top 20 songs and a massive hit with rapper Logic, and his album, *American Teen,* was in the Top 20 on *Billboard* 200 (*dont smile at me* was at 144). In May the track was further boosted by its appearance on the soundtrack to episode 13 of the second season of *13 Reasons Why* and then by being widely sampled in Juice WRLD's Top 5 album, *Goodbye & Good Riddance*.

She wore what she wanted and said exactly what she felt.

By that point the music video to "lovely" was racking up views on YouTube. Released a week after the single, it was directed by Taylor Cohen, who had previously made videos with the Saturdays and Nicki Minaj. Of course, Billie had major input into the concept, coming up with the idea of her and Khalid being trapped inside a glass box and subsumed by water and ice. A slow walking dance poignantly shows them together, but with an overwhelming feeling of loneliness.

The two singers are both dressed in black. Khalid wears a number of silver chains but is trumped by Billie, who is draped in a plethora of chains in varying lengths and weight. In New Zealand's

Sniffers magazine, she recalled how difficult it was wearing that many. "I would go to the bathroom and people would be like, "Are you OK?" she told them. "They drift one way, and I'd suddenly be walking the other way. It wasn't even just around my neck, it was around my neck, my arm, over my feet, draping all around me."

Khalid and Billie would soon be reunited as they were both on the list of artists appearing at the Governors Ball Music Festival in New York City's Randall's Island Park in June. During Billie's set she invited Khalid onstage and the two delivered an exhilarating performance of "lovely" that was acclaimed as a highlight of the festival. By this time the track had reached Number 78 in the *Billboard* Hot 100 and was making a splash around the world too. In Billie-loving Australia and New Zealand it cracked the Top 5, and in Canada, the UK, Austria, Netherlands, Norway, and Sweden it was gaining airplay and hovering around the Top 50.

In terms of chart success, "lovely" was Billie's breakthrough hit.

In terms of chart success, "lovely" was Billie's breakthrough hit. It was her first single to achieve the Hot 100, and the track received airplay and publicity beyond Billie's usual sphere, introducing her to a whole new audience. The collaboration could have been a record-company executive's dream or a publicist's masterstroke, but it wasn't. It happened because Billie and Khalid were real, were friends, and respected and valued each other's creative abilities.

CHAPTER NINE
WEARING THE CROWN

By the summer of 2018, Billie Eilish was truly on the map.

"Lovely" had nearly fifteen million views on YouTube and had been streamed 150 million times, and her Instagram following had leaped from two million to three million in the month after the single's release. Perhaps most tellingly, she was featured on the opening page of the "Vanities" section of *Vanity Fair*, which is regarded as the magazine's second cover. The section showcased artists that were on their way to the top, and in back issues Leonardo DiCaprio, Ben Affleck, Keira Knightly, Margot Robbie, Jake Gyllenhaal, and Tom Hardy had been spotlighted. With the obvious exception of Justin Bieber, few musicians had been honored, so it was a major achievement for Billie, who posed like a top model in Gucci, Fendi, and Burberry finery.

Success had enabled Billie to indulge in her passions. After a lifelong interest in clothes, she was now given access to the latest designs from top fashion houses, and her love of dance was finding an expression in music videos. In July 2018 she released a video for "hostage" through Apple Music (it would not appear on YouTube for another three months). For the video, Billie brought together some of her favorite artists. The production team was Mosaert, which comprised Stromae, a Belgian musician whose distinct style and interests mirrored her own, and his brother and artistic director Luc Junior Tam. They had produced the mesmeric Dua Lipa video for "IDGAF" along with director Henry Scholfield, who was also enlisted by Billie.

The video is a piece of contemporary dance arranged by top choreographer Matty Peacock. A two-person dance, it features an amazing male dancer called Devyck Bull (who also danced with Ariana Grande on her Dangerous Woman Tour) and Billie. Scholfield revealed that only when pushed did Billie admit to having danced before,

Billie described how she wanted the video to capture the feeling of "trying to be so close to someone that you can end up suffocating them."

but added: "She has an incredible sense of self, great ideas, and a confidence that lets her craft crazily compelling performances." This was certainly one of them, as she matches Devyck move for move, despite only recently recovering from injury.

Billie described how she wanted the video to capture the feeling of "trying to be so close to someone that you can end up suffocating them and destroying the very thing that you wanted so much." The movement between the two dancers ebbs back and forth—romantic and aggressive—as the video tells the song's story of the possessive and ultimately destructive lover. Billie asked the team to create a room equal parts intimate and suffocating, and the result was a white room with white furnishings and lighting that changes from blue to lilac and yellow. As the two protagonists dance, dressed all in white with gold chains, the room comes to life, incredibly echoing her emotions and eventually engulfing him completely. It was a great achievement, not least because it had been made while Billie was on tour. She had to learn the choreography before a show in Philadelphia, rehearse over the next couple of days as the tour went from New York to Montreal, and finally shoot it before the show in Toronto on the following day. It must have been exhausting.

Music, of course, was an enduring passion. In the early summer Billie had supported Record Store Day, the campaign to promote local record shops, by releasing a limited-edition pink-vinyl single of her ukulele-backed "party favor" along with her cover of Drake's "Hotline Bling." In interviews and posts it was clear she had a massive enthusiasm and appetite for both mainstream and under-the-radar artists. When a New Zealand YouTube video gave her $150 to spend in a record-store spree, she was like a kid in a candy store, almost unable to choose because she wanted everything.

So who better to have their own Beats 1 radio show? And what else would it be called but *Groupies Have Feelings Too*? Billie explained that the music she played was "what groupies would hear if they were with me 24/7." Over the summer of 2018, she put out six two-hour episodes. It mixed banter between Billie and Finneas with a totally eclectic mix that would surprise anyone who didn't know her. It was a total delight from the very beginning when Billie warned that "you gotta think before you speak."

Finneas responded with an astounded, "When did you ever . . . ?"

The shows were a fabulous opportunity to get to know the O'Connell siblings, as between songs they discussed anything from favorite childhood TV shows to being on tour to Billie thinking Bill and Hillary Clinton were brother and sister. And

In interviews and posts it was clear she had a massive enthusiasm and appetite for both mainstream and under-the-radar artists.

Now she was sharing the bill with her friends and heroes, and playing to thousands rather than hundreds.

then there was the music. Of course, she played her favorites like Childish Gambino, Tyler, the Creator, and J. Cole and a whole lot of hip-hop, but there were also tracks from singer-songwriters, the sixties, musical soundtracks, and lesser-known artists, including those who had shared a stage with her, like Reo Cragun and Thutmose.

For an artist ranked among the hottest new talent, the summer meant festivals. Through 2018 Billie played in the open air on many occasions, including performing at Mo Pop in Detroit, Lollapalooza in Chicago, Osheaga in Montreal, and Outside Lands in San Francisco. Now she was sharing the bill with her friends and heroes, and playing to thousands rather than hundreds. It's often difficult for solo artists to fill the massive festival stages or connect with such huge audiences, but Billie had no such problems. Standing up there, often in her bright neon suits, she seemed to have boundless energy and worked the crowd as if it was an intimate show, getting them involved, dancing, and hyped.

The large festival crowds could also be problematic. Billie's road manager, Brian Marquis, tells how at Lollapalooza Billie was struggling to walk after her performance due to a sprained ankle. She needed to get back to her hotel, so he carried her on his back. With Billie keeping her head down, he said, "I ran a city block to our hotel with kids chasing after us right into the hotel lobby, which was filled with kids from the concert," he told Pollstar. "I got her to her room and she said, 'That was fun!'"

INJURIES

"I do not know why. I am f***ing seventeen and my body is broken," Billie told the UK *Metro* newspaper. She might have the voice of an angel and a gift for songwriting, but she sure has suffered for her art. Ever since she has been in the public eye, Billie has been plagued by the kind of injuries usually reserved for sports stars. She might say she doesn't know why, but pushing her body to the limits on the dance floor as a young girl followed by a relentless schedule of tour dates as a performer might just have something to do with it.

The injury she suffered at her dance class just as "ocean eyes" had started to make waves on SoundCloud wasn't her first injury, but it was her worst yet. She was just thirteen and dancing with a group of young adults when she tore her hip flexor muscle. It was a growth-plate injury—a reasonably common affliction for active girls between the ages of thirteen and fifteen, when unhardened areas at the end of bones are vulnerable to injury. Billie's, however, was a particularly bad case where the bone separated from the muscle in her hip.

By the time she had fully recovered, she was taking her live show on the road. It is a physically demanding set, and Billie gives her all at every show. She prides herself on her ability to endure pain, so has played on through every ache and twinge, but it has taken its toll. The first major injury happened because of a stolen beanie after a show at Lollapalooza in 2018. She went wild yelling at everyone and

jumping up and down, landed wrong and badly sprained her ankle. For the rest of the tour she was forced to wear an (admittedly cool) Louis Vuitton orthopedic boot.

Audiences have become used to seeing her wearing muscle-support tape, or knee and ankle supports, and playing through pain. In Manchester, England, in February 2019 she jumped around the stage despite the agony of shin splints (later, fans would watch the livestream as she had her bandages cut off). She injured her ankle again falling down stairs before going onstage in LA in July (she went on anyway). Worse was to come when the other ankle went while jumping around at Milano Rocks in Italy in September 2019. Determined to continue the show, she performed sitting down—but the pain eventually became too much and she ran offstage in tears.

To treat her aches and pains, Billie has ongoing acupuncture, massage therapy, stretching exercises, and taping, but it seems the only thing that will stop the injuries is not going crazy onstage—and that isn't going to happen any time soon.

At Mo Pop, with no introduction, she added a new song to her set list. The crowd already knew it word for word, as "you should see me in a crown" had already been out for ten days. The lyrics came from a different side of Billie than we had seen before. She was assertive and boisterous, with her "I'm gonna run this nothing town" lines giving off a distinctly hip-hop vibe. These were undercut in the final verse by a more familiar Billie-style dark edge and the mentions of blood on the wall, sleeping in a hearse, and the phrase she confessed was her favorite: "I like the way they all scream."

The song had been premiered on Annie Mac's show on BBC Radio 1 in the UK, where Billie revealed that the title and the inspiration for the song had come from the BBC drama *Sherlock*. Finneas and Billie were big fans of the show and were watching the conclusion of the second season, "The Reichenbach Fall," in which Sherlock Holmes's evil nemesis, Jim Moriarty, who has a master key to London's high-security buildings, utters the line: "The man with the key is king—and, honey, you should see me in a crown." Billie loved the end of the quote and was determined to use it in a song. She clearly hadn't forgotten her mother's songwriting lessons and *The Walking Dead* project!

The track starts with the sound of sharpening knives (performed by Billie's dad and recorded in the kitchen) and an almost inaudible woozy synth accompanying Billie at her most whispery. It is dark and carries an ominous vibe. However, when the chorus begins, the fuzzy staccato chords and vicious beats set light to the track. As proven when debuted live at Mo Pop, the chorus has a real kick—more than enough to get a crowd moving. Through her intense touring schedule

> **It is dark and carries an ominous vibe. However, when the chorus begins, the fuzzy staccato chords and vicious beats set light to the track.**

over the previous year, Billie had learned what made a song work live and had emphasized in interviews that she was intent on creating music the audience could immerse themselves in and which she could have fun performing.

A Vevo LIFT live-performance video of the song was uploaded a few days after the release. Here the theme is luxury and opulence, and Billie sings as she dances around an empty mansion (with Finneas and Andrew in their cute $1,000 Balenciaga sweaters playing in the corner) and climbs on a massive pile of dollar bills. In an oversized white T-shirt and Louis Vuitton shorts that show off the bruises on her

A vertical Spotify video for "you should see me in a crown" appeared in August, in which Billie sang while wearing a crown covered in live spiders.

knee, Billie stomps, twists, and grooves through the song, really bringing out its energy.

Those who witnessed the Mo Pop live debut of the song were also treated to another clip from *Sherlock* on the stage's big screen. This time, it was Holmes describing Moriarty: "He's a spider. A spider at the center of a web. A criminal web with a thousand threads and he knows precisely how each and every single one of them dances." Spiders were already a thing for Billie—fans had noticed her overuse of spider emojis—but now it had become more serious . . .

A vertical Spotify video for "you should see me in a crown" appeared in August, in which Billie sang while wearing a crown covered in live spiders with other huge spiders, including tarantulas, crawling over her hands and face. So far, so bearable, but those not yet freaked out had another surprise in store. After two minutes, as Billie reaches the chorus, she opens her mouth and a huge tarantula crawls out. This was for real, not faked or CGI—and Billie had to redo the shoot a number of times to get it right. She didn't seem bothered and confessed to loving doing it. "Who knows what's wrong with me?" she joked when interrogated over the stunt.

"You should see me in a crown" soon took its place as a popular part of Billie's live set. Some in the festival crowds began to wear their own crowns to her stage, and Billie's team even took to distributing paper crowns to fans. While not reaching the heights of "lovely," the single made an impression on the charts in the US, Canada, and Europe, broke the Top 20 in Australia and, amazingly, got to Number 3 in the New Zealand charts.

Billie was now reaching out even further, flying out in August to play in South Korea and at the Japanese Summer Sonic festivals in Tokyo and Osaka. Even there she was enthusiastically greeted at the airport by screaming fans, while at the venues there were many in the audience who were able to sing along to every song. She loved the trip to Asia, especially Tokyo and Japan, where she found the designs and colors amazing. She visited the studios of artist Takashi Murakami, whose manga- and anime-influenced art she loved, and was fascinated by the Japanese fashion houses.

From her very first interviews, Billie had made no secret of her love of fashion. She had repeatedly stated her ambition to start her own clothing line, had worn outfits that she had created herself, and had mixed and matched designs from high-fashion designers. Many casual music followers knew her for her brightly colored and baggy clothes as much as for her music. So, it was no surprise to see her arriving at September 2018's New York Fashion Week in a firefighter-style orange jacket and pants.

> **From her very first interviews, Billie had made no secret of her love of fashion. She had repeatedly stated her ambition to start her own clothing line, had worn outfits that she had created herself, and had mixed and matched designs from high-fashion designers.**

Attending the Calvin Klein Collection show, she took her place in the front row alongside such luminaries as Jake Gyllenhaal, Rami Malek, Odell Beckham Jr, Mia Goth, A$AP Rocky, and her old friend Khalid. Billie was suitably thrilled to be there. "I never would have thought this would ever come at all," Billie said to fashion site WWD.com. "Since I was young, fashion has been everything in my way of expression. This was an unrealistic thing to happen, and it happened." Billie's interest in fashion was now being reciprocated. Since she had such a unique and recognizable style, and fifty million Instagram followers, the fashion industry was interested in her. Billie now officially became a model as top agency Next Models signed her up to promote fashion and beauty products.

The Wheres My Mind Tour finally ended in Washington, DC, on October 6. Back in California, she would celebrate by performing "you should see me in a crown" on *The Ellen DeGeneres Show*. Her first daytime-TV performance found Billie in a green pajama-style suit with the name Billie repeated in blue as a pattern paired with bright green high-tops. She was sat on a throne in a glass box while giant spiders were projected around her. Billie danced and prowled in a performance that would have freaked out many of the watching daytime viewers, but her fans lapped it up.

Billie had already played nearly seventy shows in 2018

Her first daytime-TV performance found Billie in a green pajama-style suit with the name Billie repeated in blue as a pattern paired with bright green high-tops. She was sat on a throne in a glass box while giant spiders were projected around her.

and was about to set off on the 1 by 1 Tour—yet another grueling city-by-city trip across the country, which would finish just in time for her seventeenth birthday. It was just as well that she lived for performing and meeting her fans, as there wasn't time for much else . . .

CHAPTER TEN
BLOHSH

By some estimates Billie's songs had been streamed a billion times by the time she set off on her new tour in October 2018.

Despite not having had a major hit outside New Zealand, she had built up an incredible fan base. A plethora of Who is this Billie Eilish? articles were now cropping up online, from rock journals to teen mags to national newspapers. The new tour would once again see her playing in bigger venues, but still to only around one thousand people each night. The shows sold out in minutes and Billie could easily have filled much larger concert halls, but her team were sticking to the plan and taking small steps to stardom.

By now, a small, slanted human figure had become associated with Billie. Their name—gender deliberately unspecified—was Blohsh (often spelled Blōhsh, with the macron mark over the "o," because it's pronounced "Blow-sh"). Blohsh started life as one of Billie's doodles, but evolved to serve as her logo, appearing on posters and much of her merchandise. Her growing success had enabled Billie to fulfill her ambition to design her own clothes.

The graphic hoodies and neon beanies in her merchandise store all began life in her sketchbook. She would download a white hoodie or a plain beanie and then color it and place the designs just where she felt they should go. Blohsh would appear as a pendant, repeated down the arm of a hoodie, or in rhinestone in the center of a T-shirt—the last a result of a collaboration with LA streetwear boutique Joyrich.

Blohsh was visible everywhere as the new tour—named the 1 by 1 Tour from a line in the "you should see me in a crown" chorus—zig-zagged its way across America. More than ever, fans assembled early, singing Billie's songs as they waited in line. Most of them were now decked out in Blohsh clothing or, failing that, in Billie-style camo pants, crops, bucket hats, or beanies. They gave a huge welcome to Finneas, who kicked off the show with a solo acoustic set, and were charged by high-energy rap act Childish Major. The sounds of Paul Anka's 1950s hit "Put Your Head on My Shoulder" and the theme from the *American Horror Story* TV show then blasted out, followed by the opening bars of "my boy" as Billie, resplendent in electric-blue hair, bounded on to the stage. Around her spread the illuminated legs of a giant spider, its body at the back of the stage doubling as a huge lighting pod.

The shows stuck to a similar format, with three short sets building up to a final moshing section that culminated with "bellyache." Each section was punctuated by some choice Billie favorites played on the PA system, including "I Got Me Some Bapes" by Soulja Boy, a Wii Games music compilation (to which Billie charmingly danced and goofed around), and Jay-Z's "Hard Knock Life (Ghetto Anthem)." Finally, every encore would turn into a raucous sing-along to "ocean eyes" and "COPYCAT." Throughout the show, Billie kept the energy levels to the maximum with her dancing (fans especially loved the synchronized dance with Finneas) and jumping around the stage. She would chat between songs, interact with the crowd, and sometimes retreat to sit on the giant spider to deliver a ballad.

Billie had chosen the very first show of the tour at the Fox Theater in Oakland, California, to introduce a special new song. As she returned to the stage for the encore, she sat at the piano and announced she was going to play a song about a friend who had recently died. She said the song was about "a powerful person that no matter what was going on in his life, he was always there for me. He made me feel OK when nothing else did." A hush came over the audience as Billie went into the tenderest of ballads. However, the tension was soon broken when a microphone fell and caused her to giggle. She then said, "We've got to get sad again," and started afresh on a heartrending song of love and loss. At the end she was hugged by Finneas as she wiped away a tear and made a cross with her arms. The crossed arms smbolized an *X* for her friend XXXTentacion and the song was titled "6.18.18," the date, almost four months ago to the day, of his death. Billie would never play the song again. Perhaps she felt she just needed to sing it once, perhaps she wanted to sidestep the controversy surrounding the rapper, but as you can see on YouTube, it is a poignant and beautiful song.

XXXTENTACION

SoundCloud rap is a genre that fuses hip-hop, trap, and rock and is incredibly popular on the streaming platform. Florida's XXXTentacion (real name Jahseh Onfroy) was one of the most popular SoundCloud rap artists. His single "Look at Me!" was uploaded to SoundCloud around the same time as "ocean eyes," when he was just seventeen, and broke into the Hot 100 in February 2017. Later that year his debut album, *17*, was a Top 10 hit in North America and across Europe, and in March 2018 his second album, *?*, went to Number 1 in the US. Just months later, on June 18, 2018, XXXTentacion, still only twenty, was fatally shot after being targeted in a robbery.

XXXTentacion's music was loved by thousands of young people, many of whom gained strength from his lyrics articulating his struggles with depression. However, there was another side to him. Both in his lyrics and life he seemed to revel in violent acts, and his songs sometimes displayed alarming misogyny. His life was dogged with controversy; he served time in juvenile detention and prison; and various charges of gun possession, violence, and domestic abuse were leveled against him.

Billie Eilish had a different view of XXXTentacion, whom she called Jah. She considered him a good friend. On the day he died, she went to Instagram to say, "All you ever did was care. i love you jah. this is so, so painful." She clearly felt he had helped her through some dark times and in a later tribute said he "was like a beam of light and just tried to do everything for other people." It was an opinion that would prove controversial as many articles and social-media comments criticized her glorification of such a violent person. Billie, however, would defend her views in an interview with the *New York Times*, saying, "I want to be able to mourn. I don't want to be shamed for it. I don't think I deserve getting hate for loving someone that passed."

ABOVE A rising star
at 2016's *Teen Vogue*
Young Hollywood event
in Malibu, California

ABOVE New York, 2017, Billie putting her heart into every performance

BELOW Billie on ukulele at the 2017 SXSW Festival in Austin, Texas

BELOW Billie and Chanel—a relationship that is still going strong

ABOVE Berlin, 2018, Billie takes every opportunity to get close to her supporters.

RIGHT Billie rocking another festival in New Hampshire

ABOVE Open and engaging, Billie once again proves the perfect interviewee.

RIGHT San Francisco, California, 2018, Billie letting loose—despite the medical boot

ABOVE United Kingdom, 2019. As ever, Billie doing it her way.

LEFT The Queen of Coachella

RIGHT Onstage at the Lowlands Festival, Netherlands, 2019

ABOVE United Kingdom, 2019, Leeds gets the full Billie festival experience.

ABOVE Billie and Finneas at the Glastonbury Festival in Pilton, Somerset, United Kingdom, in 2019

ABOVE Los Angeles, 2019, Billie with her iconic slime-green roots

ABOVE Billie and Finneas perform at the GRAMMY Museum in Los Angeles, California.

BELOW At ease backstage at the 2019 Austin City Limits Music Festival in Texas

ABOVE Winners of the 2019 American Society of Composers, Authors, and Publishers Vanguard Award for innovative music

LEFT With the Favorite Artist (Alternative Rock) trophy at the 2019 American Music Awards

LEFT Taking away the four biggest prizes at the 2020 GRAMMY Awards

BELOW Billie in full flow at the 2020 iHeartRadio ALTer EGO show

ABOVE It's all about the Burberry at the 2020 Brit Awards in London, England.

LEFT Performing the Beatles's "Yesterday" at the 2020 Academy Awards ceremony

BELOW Attending the 2020 *Vanity Fair* Oscar Party in Beverly Hills, California

ABOVE Miami, Florida, 2020, kicking off the Where Do We Go? World Tour

As the tour continued, Billie threw in some less controversial surprises. Most nights, it would take the form of a cover song on which she accompanied herself on the ukulele. Fans were treated to numbers as varied as Childish Gambino's

Despite the growing number of fans, Billie still did her best to meet as many of them as possible.

"Telegraph Ave ("Oakland" by Lloyd);" "Body Count," a cover of her friend Jessie Reyez's song; Nirvana's "Smells Like Teen Spirit;" and her childhood party piece, the Beatles's "I Will." Perhaps the sweetest moment of the tour came in Austin, Texas, when Billie brought a young fan dressed in her yellow "bellyache" outfit on to the stage. The "Mini Billie," which happened to be the girl's Instagram name, was named Elsie and was just three years old, but she delighted Billie and the crowd as she danced along to the song.

Despite the growing number of fans, Billie still did her best to meet as many of them as possible. They would thrust letters and gifts—stuffed Blohshs, home-designed T-shirts, drawings—at her, knowing she loved their creative endeavors. One particular piece of fan artwork even provided inspiration for Billie. A Montreal fan's drawing of Billie crying black tears immediately appealed to her, and she decided to use it as the basis for the "when the party's over" video, which was uploaded on October 25, 2018, a week after the single had been released.

Billie set about planning the video, and those childhood hours spent filming in her backyard were not wasted. She sat her mom by a table in the yard with a glass of water and told her to pretend to be her. Then she worked it out shot by shot, drawing and writing down every action, edit, and camera movement, before sending it to the actual director, Carlos López Estrada, who was tasked with bringing to life what would be a truly gothic nightmare.

For a brief second she stares straight at the camera before thick black tears begin to flow down her cheeks, and she then spreads them over her face and clothes.

The completed video is unique and astounding, yet so simple. Billie, sporting her dramatic blue hair, is dressed all in white with silver wrist bangles, rings, and a long chain wrapped around her neck like a necktie. She sits intently contemplating a pedestal on which rests a glass of black liquid, which she eventually gulps down. For a brief second she stares straight at the camera before thick black tears begin to flow down her cheeks, and she then spreads them over her face and clothes. In a masterful portrait of anguish and inner torment, Billie sings very few of the lines, but acts out the drama with an exquisite balance of apathy, pain, and even sensuality.

Billie had been happy to suffer for her art. First, she had to drink the glass of charcoal water mixed with xanthan gum (special effects meant at least she didn't actually have to drink the whole glass). To achieve the effect of black tears, she had tubes running up her back, over her forehead and pushed into the corner of her eyes. The black liquid was then pumped through the tubes—not just once but for six painful takes over a twelve-hour day.

"When the party's over" describes how ending a relationship can seem the right thing to do even if it hurts you. It was written by Finneas, who came up with the idea when he was driving home alone, having suddenly decided to leave the house of a girl he was dating. Since the beginning of the year, it had been a staple of the live set, when Billie would sing to Finneas's piano accompaniment, but the studio version was highly produced and textured. The piano sound was less evident, but Billie's layered voice created a wall of emotion.

Finneas wrote on Twitter that they knew they had to do something unforgettable with it, since so many fans knew the song already. He said how hard it was to record as they built it up using hundreds of vocal layers. On Instagram, when Billie posted the artwork, a sketch by acclaimed Swiss tattoo artist Manuela Soto Sosa of a young girl crying, she said how the track had been "impossible to record." Later, she would tell *Fader* magazine that it took ninety takes just to get the first word, "Don't," to sound how she wanted it to.

The production, along with the video and the growing awareness of Billie as an accomplished artist, ensured that "when the party's over" was her most successful single to date. It reached Number 29 on the Hot 100, Number 21 in the UK charts, and made the Top 10 in Norway, Sweden, Ireland, and Estonia, as well as in the ever-loyal Canada, Australia, and New Zealand.

The production, along with the video and the growing awareness of Billie as an accomplished artist, ensured that "when the party's over" was her most successful single to date.

"When the party's over" was featured in another Vevo LIFT recording. This gave a taste of the 1 by 1 Tour with a live performance recorded in November in Brooklyn, New York. It was an intimate show on a white rectangular stage in the middle of a small but pumped audience that was given space to dance. Finneas and Andrew were in their repeated-Billie-motif outfits while Billie wore an oversized black-and-white checked Chanel tracksuit. Along with the new single, they played "bellyache" and "when the party's over" in the short set, which many declared was among Billie's best-ever live performances. The sound is top quality; Billie sings perfectly and seems energized by the freedom of the encircled stage and the receptive audience of enthusiastic fans, who yelp and scream between songs but allow her voice to be heard.

On November 20, the tour finale brought Billie back to LA for a three-night celebration at the historic Fonda Theatre on Hollywood Boulevard. However, she had one more local booking earlier that day, in nearby Santa Monica. In a well-kept secret, Billie and Finneas launched a new track called "come out and play," performing it to a small, seated audience in the Apple Store. Warm and sweet with a lullaby feel, the song finds Billie singing to an acoustic guitar and a soft beat with a slowly rising crescendo. The words "Don't hide" are repeated in the chorus: the most direct Billie gets in terms of gently persuading listeners to show their true selves.

The Apple connection was that the song was the soundtrack to the company's holiday TV commercial, set to be broadcast over the forthcoming Thanksgiving holiday and in the weeks up to Christmas. The ad itself—part of the Share Your Gifts campaign—was delightful. The Pixar-style animation painted a beautiful winter scene and focused on a curly-haired, freckle-faced young woman who kept hiding her creative talents. Eventually, thanks to her big shaggy dog, her carefully locked-away illustrations are taken by a gust of wind and distributed to passersby who, of course, are appreciative and deeply impressed. Because of their ties with Apple, Billie and Finneas had been sent a very early version of the animation

The theme of being proud of your creativity was perfect for Billie.

and asked to write a fitting song as a soundtrack. The theme of being proud of your creativity was perfect for Billie, but she cleverly expanded the idea to a reassurance for those suffering from social anxiety.

They played the track again that evening at the Fonda Theatre, but it was overshadowed by another appearance from Khalid. This time, not only did he and Billie sing "lovely" together, but she also joined him for a duet of his "Young Dumb & Broke" hit. Nevertheless, "come out and play" was an immediate crowd favorite; the commercial brought Billie's voice to thousands who hadn't heard it yet, and the song joined "when the party's over" in charts around the world.

In October, Billie had played a couple of concerts as an opening act for Florence and the Machine in the US. They had gone well, with the two acts complementing each other and the audience appreciating Billie's set. The plan was for Billie to rejoin Florence and the Machine's High as Hope Tour in Australia in the New Year, but in December it was announced that Billie was withdrawing due to "international scheduling conflicts." It seemed puzzling as Billie had no concerts planned until her European tour began in February, but she herself was more forthcoming, writing on Twitter that "unfortunately we all came to realize recently that we need some more time to finish something very important before going back out and doing more shows." Her fans had a good idea what that something might be. She had been promising a full album for some time, and here was the biggest hint that it was imminent.

CHAPTER ELEVEN

THE MONSTER UNDER THE BED

I was totally silent and totally still and tears just streamed down my face.

In her famous *Vanity Fair* annual interview, that was how Billie Eilish recalled reacting to first seeing her schedule for the forthcoming year. In January 2019 she had six million Instagram followers and had recently been selected as one of a handful of teenagers on the prestigious *Forbes* 30 Under 30 list, which recognizes young business and industry highfliers. She was the youngest-ever artist to top a billion spins on Spotify, and "ocean eyes" had entered the Top 100 in the US and the UK, a full year after release. Now she was looking at a list of over one hundred concerts, including some of the biggest festivals in the world.

Billie had turned seventeen two weeks earlier, celebrating her birthday with family and friends at an ice-skating rink (she hired the whole rink because she couldn't go without being mobbed—and she missed skating!). No wonder she felt overwhelmed. She was still a teenager. In her Instagram videos she dances and goofs around with people her own age, something she must have missed out on so much as she spent her younger teens touring, giving interviews, and recording—essentially working.

At the end of 2018, Billie had bought herself a present—her first car. Eschewing BMWs and Mercedes and the other pop-star vehicles of choice, Billie bought a matte-black Dodge Challenger, the car she had been obsessed with since she was twelve and that she had insisted on having in her "watch" video. "It's my best friend, my girlfriend . . . I call it The Dragon, after my favorite mythical animal," she told *Vogue* magazine, before adding, "My mom made sure it has all the best safety features." She needed Maggie's approval because an adult was still legally required to sit with her while she drove—Billie wouldn't get her full license until the summer. Nevertheless, she would proudly pose with it for photos and boasted of driving it alone, even if it was just to park it around the back of the house.

Billie bought a matte-black Dodge Challenger, the car she had been obsessed with since she was twelve and that she had insisted on having in her "watch" video.

Nobody was expecting to hear much from Billie in January. She had canceled the Florence and the Machine concerts in Australia, and the European tour would not start until February. It was clear that the month had been put aside to complete work on her long-awaited debut album, so it came as a great surprise on January 8, 2019, when, through Instagram, she teased a new song due to be released the following day. The track was called "WHEN I WAS OLDER" and the cover art said it was inspired by the movie *Roma* and featured a scene from the movie, showing a young woman on the beach running toward the sea.

Roma had been the hit movie of the winter in theaters and on Netflix, and was nominated for ten Oscars (at the ceremony in February, it would win three). The movie followed the tough

Most reviewers considered "WHEN I WAS OLDER" to be the pick of the tracks on *Music Inspired by the Film Roma*.

but quietly endured life of Cleo, a young live-in maid in Mexico City in the early 1970s. The enthralling, emotional, and intimate portrait mirrored the style of many of Billie's songs, so an invite from *Roma*'s director, Alfonso Cuarón, to contribute a song to an album of music inspired by the movie made complete sense.

In *Roma*, Pepe, a young boy prone to fantasizing about previous lives, utters the line, "When I was older I used to be a sailor, but I drowned in a storm." Billie and Finneas took the first part of that line, and images from the movie, and created a song and soundscape that retains the essence of *Roma*. Billie's silky but melancholic, introspective vocals (with a rare use of autotune) perfectly capture Cleo's mood, while Finneas is in his element as he samples student protest chants, a dog barking, and the sounds of ocean waves and raging fires from the soundtrack in a haunting, minimalist instrumental. "Nothing about this song would exist without the film," they said, "which is exactly what we love about it."

Most reviewers considered "WHEN I WAS OLDER" to be the standout track on *Music Inspired by the Film Roma*, which was quite a compliment considering renowned artists such as Patti Smith and Beck had also contributed. While not reaching the heights of her recent singles, it was well received and kept fans happy while they awaited the big news. Billie kept them in suspense. On January 13, she captioned a photo on Instagram saying "mastering the album today" and then, three days later, she posted a single word: "March."

On February 28, Billie went on Twitter, YouTube, and Instagram to announce the title of the new album, which was to be called *When We All Fall Asleep, Where Do We Go?* She also shared a sixteen-second teaser video of her singing a new song, which ended in the album title. The brief video was somewhat alarming, though, with Billie singing while black-gloved hands grabbed at her head, face, and neck. The following day another post appeared, this time alongside a ghoulish photo of Billie in all white, sitting on an unmade white bed in a spotlight. With her white bulging eyes and unnerving grin, the image looked as if it had come straight from a horror movie. The message repeated the album title and promised a new song the next morning.

Although she writes from the perspective of the tormenting beast, it is sometimes unclear who is being tormented.

After the short wait, "bury a friend"—a track that Billie herself would describe as an incredibly weird song—was revealed. Written by Finneas and Billie in a couple of free days after their Lollapalooza performance on Finneas's twenty-first birthday, it is a disjointed but atmospheric and surprisingly catchy piece. Perhaps influenced by the pain Billie was in after injuring her ankle, it hints at cruelty and violence, but has an almost playful, childlike feel. The instrumental track reflects this with a jaunty shuffle beat interspersed with the sound of drills recorded during an orthodontist appointment, screams, and other disconcerting noises.

The lyrics are based around the concept of the monster under the bed. Billie's starting point for the whole song was a drawing she made of a monster, and although she writes from the perspective of the tormenting beast, it is sometimes unclear who is being tormented. Like the instrumental track, the song's words are littered with horror allusions, but also reverberate with self-doubt and despair. The final piece of the jigsaw is supplied by Billie's delivery: semiwhispered with stilted and sometimes childlike pronunciation (the perfectly affected "ashleep," for example) with vocal echoes that enhance the haunting atmosphere.

MEHKI RAINE

Early in the writing of "bury a friend," Billie decided she needed a voice calling her name to jolt the song into action. She also knew whose voice she needed: her friend Calvin's. A rapper from London, Calvin Parkinson first went under the name of Crooks and then Mehki Raine. Billie came across him on Instagram, as he kept tagging her in his photos and asking, "Where's Billie at?" She thought he was cute and funny, and they became good friends.

When asked to choose her best albums of 2018 for *Billboard* magazine, Billie had picked *Dog Eat Dog World*, the album by Mehki Raine (although she was still calling him Crooks). She remarks on his deep British voice, but it is clear how the unsettling low-key production, unorthodox rapping style, and poetic word play would also appeal to her. *Dog Eat Dog World* has since racked up over forty thousand spins, with Mehki Raine's 2019 album *Black Sheep* also being well received.

The video for "bury a friend" was released on the same day as the single. Once Michael Chaves was enlisted as director, the course it was going to take was clear. Chaves's short film *The Maiden* had won the Best Super Short Horror Film Award at Shriekfest and his scary movie *The Curse of La Llorona* was showing in theaters as they made the video. Of course, Billie brought her own ideas to the party. She sketched out the nightmare scenario, and Chaves delivered with a video that was reminiscent of late-night horror movies.

Calvin was flown over to play the sleeping figure who calls her name, while Billie plays the monster under the bed. She is dressed in white shirt and pants that are definitely Billie-style but also project an image of asylum inmates. It is a disturbing vision; her blacked-out eyes in the under-the-bed scenes are creepy, and the images of her naked back pierced by a dozen syringes and her juddering, suspended feet are truly scary.

In its first twenty-four hours the "bury a friend" video racked up more than thirteen million views on YouTube, with the single receiving four million spins on Spotify. In fact, the single made an immediate impact all around the world. This time, it wasn't just in Canada, Australia, and New Zealand that it made the Top 3, but in Scandinavia and eastern Europe too. It became Billie's first Top 10 hit

In its first twenty-four hours the "bury a friend" video racked up more than thirteen million views on YouTube.

in the UK and reached 14 in the US, her highest position yet on the *Billboard* 100. She was even making an impression in Asia, registering on charts in Malaysia, Japan, and South Korea.

It was the perfect time for Billie to set out on the road again as she took her 1 by 1 Tour to Europe for seventeen sold-out dates.

She gave "bury a friend" a live debut at the first date at the Kesselhaus in Berlin, and it was immediately apparent that it was to be a crowd favorite. As with so many of their other songs, she and Finneas managed to turn an intense, quiet

The fans played their part too. They already knew every word and provided backing vocals, taking great pleasure in bawling the "I wanna end me" line.

track into a stage stomper brimming with energy. The fans played their part too. They already knew every word and provided backing vocals, taking great pleasure in bawling the "I wanna end me" line. "WHEN I WAS OLDER" was also included in the set list for the first time. Although the live arrangement of the song was similar to the subdued recorded version, Billie still found an opportunity to dance around the stage during the break.

The tour progressed through Denmark, Sweden, France, Italy, Switzerland, the Netherlands, and Belgium. Everywhere she went, it was the same. She was still playing standing-only venues to excited crowds, mainly of teenage girls with a sprinkling of boys and older fans, packed in front of the stage while chaperoning parents hung back. The whole show would be like karaoke, and Billie joked that she could just lie motionless on the stage (or even not turn up) and they would still have the time of their lives.

Billie did her meet and greets in every city, interacting with as many fans as she could, and then she would climb onstage to give it her all. And yet, she later confided, for someone on the cusp of being a global superstar, these were dark times indeed. She referred to the tour in Europe as her lowest point. She had seen what fame had done to other young performers and worried she was going to have a breakdown. Thankfully, she managed to get through the tour and found herself in a better place.

By the end of February the tour had reached the UK. Her first stop was the legendary Maida Vale Studios in London, where everyone from the Beatles to David Bowie and Nirvana to the White Stripes had played for the BBC. She was there to record six songs for BBC DJ Annie Mac, a supporter of Billie since the early "ocean eyes" days. Billie, for the most part seated on a stool, wore a black-and-white skeleton hoodie with black shorts and a fistful of gold rings (including a stunning snake ring). In this short set, with Finneas and Andrew playing behind her, she performed a different version of their songs. It was neither the energized live style nor the stripped-back acoustic versions but instead a softer version of the recorded releases, with Billie's vocals at the fore.

> **Billie, for the most part seated on a stool, wore a black-and-white skeleton hoodie with black shorts and a fistful of gold rings.**

This was a performance ranked among her best by many fans, especially as it included a previously unheard number, a cover of Phantogram's 2016 hit "You Don't Get Me High Anymore," which Billie introduced as "one of [her] favorite songs of all time." The original, a pounding electro-rock track, is slowed down so that Billie can beautifully but agonizingly pull out the frustration that nothing is good enough, and it translates perfectly. Perhaps the biggest compliment was that it sounded just like one of her and Finneas's songs.

Midway through the 1 by 1 Tour of the UK, "wish you were gay" was released as the fourth single from the forthcoming album. Although Billie had been playing the song regularly in live shows since it was first heard on the livestream in June 2017, this was the first time it had been issued officially. The single keeps the original acoustic guitar but adds an insistent slap beat and brings in a synth punch to build a crescendo. Although it is a hurting song, trying to salvage pride in the face of rejection, it is also playful, especially with the clever countdown contained in the lyrics.

The single maintained Billie's profile in the charts, but not all the reaction was positive. Some members of the LGBTQ community did take offense. Since she had first played the song live, Billie had been aware that some people might not interpret the song in the way that she'd meant it. In June 2018 she had gone on Instagram to explain and defend it, saying that it's "so not meant to be offensive in any way. It literally means I wish he was gay so that he didn't like me for an actual reason." To back up her case she had even decided to donate some proceeds from her Blohsh apparel line to the Trevor Project, the world's largest suicide and crisis prevention program for at-risk LGBTQ youth.

Before they left the UK, Billie and Finneas played one special acoustic show at the intimate Pryzm club just outside London. The small, all-age audience was made up of competition winners. They were dedicated fans, and Billie was genuinely thrilled to be playing for them. The connection between an artist and their supporters can rarely have been so close. When Billie talked of having recurring nightmares where they stop liking her, they responded with so much warmth and love, and when the show came to a close, she couldn't bring herself

She had gone on Instagram to explain and defend it, saying that it's "so not meant to be offensive in any way. It literally means I wish he was gay so that he didn't like me for an actual reason."

They must all have felt exhausted after finishing such an intense tour, but they were about to embark on the biggest adventure so far.

to leave the stage, but dived head-first into the front three rows and tried to hug them all.

Heading home in March 2019, Billie and her team stopped off in Barcelona for the final show of the tour. In the audience that night was the Catalan singer Rosalía. Although Rosalía is eight years older than Billie, they had much in common. They shared a creative spirit nurtured in bedroom recordings, so-called overnight stardom that actually took years of hard work, and a reputation for saying exactly what they thought. Rosalía had taken flamenco to new levels, fusing it with R & B, and had become a massive star of Latin pop, even being dubbed the Rihanna of Flamenco. In 2018 she had a breakthrough hit with "Malamente" and was about to release "Con Altura," a collaboration with reggaeton star J Balvin that would be an international chart-topper.

In an interview accompanying the Annie Mac recordings, Billie revealed she had already met up for a studio session with Rosalía a month earlier. She talked of singing really high harmonies and said she had sung "some notes I had never even thought about." She clearly liked the Latin singer, saying that she really knows what she wants and that she'd thought, "Wow, you're the only other person I've really met that's like this." After seeing Billie's show in Barcelona, Rosalía tweeted that "seeing you perform inspired me sooo much" and tellingly teased that she couldn't wait to finish their song. To date, it is still to be released, but fans still hope to hear them sing together sometime soon.

As Billie and her team returned to California, it must have felt so strange. They had received a rapturous welcome in every country they had visited and played shows at large venues, yet every hall could have been filled ten times over and she was getting more and more popular by the day. Similarly, they must all have felt exhausted after finishing such an intense tour, but they were about to embark on the biggest adventure so far—the launch of a debut album and a world tour. It was enough to bring anyone to tears.

CHAPTER TWELVE
FOURTEEN PIECES OF ART

With only two weeks to go before the release of one of the most highly anticipated albums in years, Billie's return to the SXSW Festival in March 2019 created an expectant buzz.

In Austin she headlined the festival, playing the Uber Eats House, the very same venue where she and Finneas had played on the patio two years previously. It was a small, twenty-one-plus show, and there were plenty of music-industry VIPs present. "I know you guys are over twenty-one," Billie joked, "but you still know how to jump, right?"—and indeed many older Billie fans proved they could be just as loud and knew just as many words as the younger fans did. The stage show was still evolving: Billie had mastered how to have an audience eating out of her hand from the get-go; the fierce lighting system added excitement and atmosphere; and now they had added a massive screen that played high-definition videos behind her while she sang.

Visuals had always been prominent in Billie's mind in her songs and performances. Now she had the means to fully express them and she grasped every opportunity. When she was in Japan, she had met artist Takashi Murakami, who she called an "incredible visionary," and a collaboration was born. His animation skills were combined with her

> **Visuals had always been prominent in Billie's mind in her songs and performances.**

vivid imagination, and after eight months' work, the result was a second official video for "you should see me in a crown" (the first being the version with the spider in her mouth). The anime-style, neon-colored animation takes Billie from performing on a stage to a familiar nightmare scenario inhabited by grotesque monsters and a giant spider. It incorporates both Billie's Blohsh figures and Murakami's signature colorful flower icons, and is clearly driven by Billie's vision with Murakami's talents emerging through the caricature and movement of animated Billie and the way he brings the scene to life.

On March 28, the eve of the release date, Billie went on the *Jimmy Kimmel Live!* show in the US, where she performed "bury a friend." Once again, she showed that to make an impression she did not have to perform to fans who had been listening to her music on repeat. The late-night show audience was clearly captivated by her short but devastating set. Even as the intro started up, she was jumping and striding around the stage, dressed in a black top that spelled out "DIE" in dripping-blood-style wool threads and shorts with similar threads and "smiley" faces with black flowing from their eyes. The set gave off a spooky feel as dry ice swirled around a white bed, but then at the midsong break a sheet fell behind Billie. Finneas and Andrew continued to play in silhouette from behind the sheet, but disappeared as the shape of a monster shadow appeared. It was a superb spectacle, and given the way Billie ended the song—with an impassioned yell of the album title—it seemed she knew it too. As a last performance before her life changed forever, it was a pretty good one.

"Bury a friend" was an apt song to perform just hours before the album dropped. When they made that song, it inspired not only the concept and visuals but also how Billie wanted the work to be perceived. The album had been three years in the making, and yet it was the question posed in "bury a friend" that tied it together; every song, Billie said, asks the question: When we all fall asleep, where do we go? She explained that many songs on the album derived from nightmares, super-real dreams, or even sleep paralysis (when you wake from sleep but feel paralyzed and may hallucinate), a frightening state that Billie claimed to have experienced five times.

The album was not a selection of songs thrown together, but a carefully considered collection of tracks that worked individually yet fed into and off one another. Billie described the tracks as "fourteen pieces of art" to DJ Annie Mac; but, speaking to *Tidal* magazine, she also explained how the album made sense as one piece of art. Musically, there are jumps from genre to genre, and lyrically the subject and perspective changes with each song, but there is an overriding sensibility—an authenticity and darkness—that links them.

> **Every song, Billie said, asks the question: When we all fall asleep, where do we go?**

Billie and Finneas had been creating the songs specifically for the album (incredibly, still recording in his bedroom) and both of them talked about it with immense pride. For a seventeen-year-old (and a twenty-one-year-old) it was an extraordinary achievement. Billie loved it so much that, during the *Jimmy Kimmel Live!* recordings, made the night before the album dropped, she supposedly wobbled and had to be talked out of canceling the release by a member of her team. It was her baby, which she and Finneas had loved and nurtured, and you could understand her misgivings about sending it out to face judgment by the world.

When We All Fall Asleep, Where Do We Go? features the four singles: "you should see me in a crown," "wish you were gay," "when the party's over," and "bury a friend." Dedicated fans may also have been familiar with an early version of "8" and "listen before i go," which had been played live at many shows. That still left eight brand-new tracks. Or maybe seven, because the first track, "!!!!!!!," lasts just fourteen seconds. The opening track is actually an afterthought. Having completed the album, Finneas and Billie decided it needed something more to offset the darkness of many of the songs. They used this short dialogue around a running joke they shared about Billie taking out her Invisaligns (clear braces) before singing. Comparing the noise her doing this made to the signature cigarette-lighter-flick sound that begins rapper Lil Wayne's tracks, they would joke about how the sound of her removing her Invisaligns could become Billie's own signature.

"Bad guy" was always going to be the album's actual opener, even before any of the other track listings had been worked out. It's easy to see why. If in some of their previous tracks they had shown a seed of pop genius, then "bad guy" is when it blossoms. Finneas's production is clinical, and he exhibits fantastic control over the samples and the sound, while Billie's vocals smoothly coast from sweet to sarcastic to threatening. The tune is infectious from the start, with a walking bassline augmented by a simple beat and finger clicks that feed into a perfect sing-along chorus—that has no words. After the success of "bury a friend," Finneas declared that if they could get away with demolishing the structure of a song like that, they could do anything. And here they do, with not only a vocal-free chorus but also with a break forty seconds before the end of the song at which point the tempo, tune, and mood change completely—meaning that, in effect, they finish the track with a different song.

Billie's lyrics for "bad guy" are smart, witty, and charming and almost insist on being sung along to. As she alternates between being playful and flirtatious, and sardonic and cruel, the lyrics brilliantly ridicule the male tough-guy image. However, as she trips out rhyme after rhyme, she undercuts her own argument with boasts and the glorious "Duh" that ends the prechorus. All in all, it adds up to a three-minute diatribe against fake personas that manages to be simultaneously fun and cutting.

Next up is "xanny." Billie doesn't always write from firsthand experience or her own point of view, but she makes it clear that this song about her friends' drugs, cigarettes, and alcohol use is personal. As an onlooker, she describes these habits as selfish, irrational, boring, and life-reducing (in terms of both fun and health). The song's verse and chorus are distinctly different: the chorus is filled with disconcerting distortion, while the verse, with its tinkling piano and sultry delivery, brings to mind a smoky jazz club and the crooning of a singer like Ella Fitzgerald. In "A Snippet into Billie's Mind," a short series on her YouTube channel in which she talks about some of the songs, Billie explains that "the verses are like what smoke looks like and the choruses are like what it feels like."

After "you should see me in a crown" comes another piano-based track in "all the good girls go to hell." This time, it is played up-tempo, taking the song into the realm of pop. With Billie interrupting her own semi-spoken delivery with bursts of sweet-sung melody, the track teases with the idea of letting loose but ultimately stays on the restrained side. Peppered with intriguing and ambiguous lines, the song hints at man replacing the devil as God's foe as we doom ourselves through the destruction of our Earth, and images of hills burning, waters rising, trees disappearing, and waters or our air being poisoned powerfully express the theme of climate change.

Images of hills burning, waters rising, trees disappearing, and waters or our air being poisoned powerfully express the theme of climate change.

"Wish you were gay" and "when the party's over" take the album to the halfway mark, and then in "8," we reach the oldest of the tracks. Back in August 2017, the song was played on the livestream and became known as "see-through." Billie and Finneas didn't seem to like that title, though, and called it "8" because it was the eighth song on the album (it was called "7" until they added "!!!!!!!" as a separate track at the front). The rejected-lover song, which Billie had written from the perspective of someone she had spurned, had been given the Finneas touch. He had played with her vocal and ukulele sound, speeding it up to give the achingly raw song of the livestream a boost of energy and a more quirky feel.

"My strange addiction" and "ilomilo," sandwiched either side of "bury a friend," both feature Billie wearing her Gen Z credentials on her sleeve. The first has a delicious bass-guitar note as a beat and develops into a seventies disco-sounding chorus. Written by Finneas, it is a song about an addiction to a person, but typically Billie hijacks the meaning with inserts from her favorite TV comedy series, *The Office*. They needed the writer's and cast's approval, which was readily given, with B. J. Novak, star and writer of the series, saying, "I was like, wow, bonus, this is a banger."

"Ilomilo" is an altogether different kind of song, but it references something many of her teen fans would recognize. *Ilomilo* was a cute video game that involved reuniting two characters who separate and fear they will never find each other again. In the song, Billie takes the idea and runs with it, letting her mind spin over love and the fear of loss. The insistent pulse, skipping notes (and echoes of the game's sound effects), along with vocals that feel so tense they are at a breaking point, make for an intriguing and beguiling track. It is so far from being filler—and, indeed, Billie would sometimes name "ilomilo" as her favorite song.

The next track was never completed and therefore wasn't included. "I don't know, i just wish i wasn't breathing" was due to come before "listen before i go," "i love you," and "goodbye," which when read together made a sentence, but nevertheless the sentiment remained. Of the new tracks, "i love you" proves that Billie and Finneas can write a traditional ballad when they choose. Accompanied by a gentle acoustic guitar, the lyrics, which try and fail to deny love, are deft and poetic (with a cadence that brings Leonard Cohen's "Hallelujah" to mind), while Billie's voice exudes a tenderness that is absent from most of her songs.

Billie told MTV News, "I don't like when a song just ends an album and then nothing feels like it's actually over." She was determined that her last song would have a sense of finality; so, taking "Please, don't leave me be" from the backing vocals of "xanny," she then picked a line from every single song on the album, from last to first. "When it gets to the top," she added, "it just kind of dies down and it feels like it's a

She was determined that her last song would have a sense of finality.

goodbye. It almost feels like an RIP." Even if you don't realize this, the two-minute song stands alone and has a lullaby feel, which is, as ever, undercut by Billie with the final line of "I'm the bad guy."

BILLIE AND SYNESTHESIA

Synesthesia is the blending of one sense with another. It can involve any of the senses, so a smell can be associated with a color or the feel of an object with a sight. It is a technique used by writers and poets, but some people experience it involuntarily and constantly. Associations can be random, such as people with numbers or the taste of honey with a certain song, but the perceptions are permanent; the same number always comes to mind with a certain person or honey whenever you hear that song played.

Both Billie and Finneas experience synesthesia. Billie has said that everyone she knows has not only their own number, but their own color and shape in her head too. This goes some way to explaining her visual approach to songwriting. In a YouTube music video she explained how "everything that I make, I'm already thinking of what color it is, and what texture it is, and what day of the week it is, and what number it is, and what shape." She has described "bad guy" as yellow but also red, the number seven, hot, but warm, like an oven and smelling like cookies; and talked of "xanny" as velvety with the feeling of smoke.

The Billie Eilish Experience pop-up in Los Angeles was timed to coincide with the album release. It enabled fans to see her music how she sees it, by giving each song on the album its own room with a distinct temperature, number, color, shape, texture, and smell. They could experience each song, from racing toy cars around a course of cookie dough and vegan milk in the "bad guy" room to the puppies in the "8" room and the throbbing bass in the uncomfortable, smoke-filled "xanny" room.

Billie once claimed that her music is "all about comfort and it's about 'I know how you're feeling and you are not alone.'" As media commentators almost unanimously praised the album, they picked up on how well her lyrics reflected the teenage sensibility and the attitudes of Gen Z and millennials to the world around them. They recognized how Billie and Finneas had succeeded in producing a cohesive piece of work with its own unity, and how easily they moved across genres and created totally different songs. Some even credited the album with breaking down boundaries in pop music, which was praise indeed for a collection recorded in a bedroom and a series of hotel rooms.

CHAPTER THIRTEEN

FESTIVAL GIRL

Billie's "bad guy" video took everyone aback. She'd done weird and freaky before, but she was pushing it further and further.

Like the song itself, the video was part humorous, part self-mocking, part scathing, and more than a little disturbing— and it hit the sweet spot. It received over 7.5 million views in just twenty-four hours and 35 million in its first week.

Billie had turned to Dave Meyers to direct the video. Meyers was the best in the business. He had worked on videos for Taylor Swift, Ariana Grande, Katy Perry, and Travis Scott; had won GRAMMYs for Kendrick Lamar's "Humble" and Missy Elliott's "Lose Control;" and earlier in the year had directed "Señorita" for Shawn Mendes and Camila Cabello. He had a reputation for collaborating with artists and allowing their personality to shine through.

In the "bad guy" video Meyers's love of color blocking, bold imagery, and stunning backdrops is evident, but so is Billie's imagination and visual creativity. The two came together in the stunning set pieces that are so skillfully edited together. Billie's ungainly entry through a yellow paper wall, her gang cruising down the road on tiny tricycles, the milk being poured into a man's mouth in the middle of a red desert and, of course, the enduring images of Billie nonchalantly singing with blood smeared on her face, sitting cross-legged on a guy's back while he does push-ups or, weirdest of all, the heads hanging in plastic bags.

The video helped catapult "bad guy" to the top of charts in over a dozen countries across the world, from Australia to Iceland, and into the Top 10 in as many again, including the UK, Japan, and Brazil. In the US, after nine weeks at Number 2, it finally displaced Lil Nas X's "Old Town Road" to gain the top spot. Not only did he send her a congratulatory tweet, but Billie achieved the distinction of being the first artist born in the twenty-first century to have a Number 1 on the *Billboard* Hot 100.

When We All Fall Asleep, Where Do We Go? was running away to similar success, matching or even surpassing the single's chart placing. In the UK she became the youngest-ever solo female act to top the album chart, while the album went straight to Number 1 on the *Billboard* 200 (it would return to the top twice more), with *Forbes* deducing that its fourteen songs were streamed 194 million times in the first seven days after release. It must have been beyond Billie and Finneas's wildest dreams. With an album recorded in his tiny bedroom, they had instantly joined the ranks of Drake, Ariana, and Cardi B.

> **It must have been beyond Billie and Finneas's wildest dreams. With an album recorded in his tiny bedroom, they had instantly joined the ranks of Drake, Ariana, and Cardi B.**

If Billie was the new queen of pop, she needed a coronation—and where better to be crowned than at Coachella?

If Billie was the new queen of pop, she needed a coronation— and where better to be crowned than at Coachella, perhaps the most famous music festival in the world? On two consecutive weekends in April around one hundred thousand people flock to the Colorado Desert festival in California to see pop, rock, and dance music's biggest acts. Despite growing up just a two-hour drive from the festival, Billie had never been able to afford a ticket. Until a year previously, she hadn't envisioned ever being successful enough to play the festival. Yet here she was with a Number 1 hit as the most anticipated act on the bill.

Despite Billie's meteoric rise to fame, she had been booked on the smaller second stage, the Outdoor Theatre. That meant a crush at the gates and even in the VIP area to see what was so special about this teenage sensation. At first, a technical problem with the big screen behind the stage delayed her appearance, heightening the tension, and the crowd started chanting her name—but after half an hour some frustrated fans began to trickle away. However, five minutes later, they hurried back. The screen had come alive, flashing with scary silhouettes and creepy images that eventually framed the real-life Billie. Her hair was now dark, and she was dressed all in white—a Siberia Hills hoodie, baggy shorts down to her calves, socks, and high-tops.

It's no exaggeration to say that within the hour Billie owned the festival. She began her set with the first-ever live performance of "bad guy," the audience a sea of bodies jumping in unison, waving their arms and often drowning her out with their singing. She then swept into "my strange addiction" as images of Blohsh flashed on the now-working screen, and went on to debut "all the good girls go to hell" and "ilomilo" in a performance that took

She had that massive audience—who even knew every word of songs she had released just two weeks earlier—in the palm of her hand.

the breath away. She had that massive audience—who even knew every word of songs she had released just two weeks earlier—in the palm of her hand. They leaped when she leaped, sung along intently to her ballads, and delighted in the unexpected, such as the twitching bedridden dancers or when she ghoulishly stood on a levitating bed to sing "bury a friend."

When she forgot the words in the second verse of "all the good girls go to hell," she styled it out so coolly that it endeared the audience to her even more. Even when Vince Staples's microphone failed to work during "&burn," no one seemed to care. Not least her new celebrity fans—Kylie Jenner, Travis Scott, members of 5 Seconds of Summer, Katy Perry, and Lady Gaga—watching from the guest area or, in Bruno Mars's case, on TV as he tweeted "@billieeilish I'm seeing these live clips and you're killin! A vibe like that at 17? Sheesh." No wonder fans were calling for the festival, which the press had dubbed Beychella following Beyoncé's 2018 performance, to be renamed Billiechella!

The next weekend she did it all again, this time with Justin and Hailey Bieber, Jaden Smith, and members of Blackpink in the audience. High winds meant there was no floating bed, but the show was slicker. Billie had switched to an all-black outfit, including a (soon-to-be iconic) freaky neon "Joker" T-shirt from the NYC brand Bond. To headline Coachella, let alone smash it out of the park, was a big, big deal for Billie. She took it all in her stride, performing like a seasoned professional, but just occasionally the enormity of her achievement seemed to dawn on her and she was that seventeen-year-old again. At one point, as her fans screamed out their love, she told them, "I literally used to sit in my room and cry because I wanted this s*** so bad." Later, she wiped away tears and told them, "I promise you, if I could stay up on this stage for the rest of my life I would. Forever." She added: "I feel like I'm not here. Like this isn't real."

JUSTIN BIEBER

"I saw [him]. I know what Bieber looks [like]. I know his body language. I know how he stands. I know where he wears his pants," she told James Corden as they went on their "Carpool Karaoke" trip. "So I look over and he just stood there. Like five feet away from me. Perfectly still. And he had the face mask so all I could see were his eyes." Billie was recalling the moment at Coachella where she had met her fangirl crush, Justin Bieber.

Billie had made no secret of how big a Belieber she once was. Before, but not so long before "ocean eyes," her bedroom had been covered with posters of the Canadian pop star and a sign on her bedroom door read, "Forever Belieber, Billie's room." In a video made when she was twelve she even says how she is worried that when she gets a boyfriend, she won't want to be with him because she actually loves Justin.

In March 2019, the two stars' orbits had moved closer when she revealed that he had started following her on social media—sending a screenshot of a DM she had sent him in 2014—as she prepared to go on *The Ellen DeGeneres Show*. On the program she made it clear that he still meant a lot to her and seemed visibly nervous that he would appear as a surprise guest. He didn't, but a month later, in the California desert, here they were, hugging like long-lost friends and dancing together as NSYNC performed with Ariana Grande.

They were now good buddies. Bieber provided a rap-style verse to a remix of "bad guy" in July and to celebrate Billie shared a picture of her at twelve, dressed in a rainbow ballet dress, standing in front of her poster-adorned wall. The remix was seen as taking the edge off the original, but it was fun and still sold well, with fans loving the novelty.

Their friendship made headlines again in February 2020, when a tearful Bieber recalled the difficulties he'd experienced being a teenage star and told Beats 1 that he wanted to help Billie avoid going through the same things. "If she ever needs me I'm going to be here for her," he told listeners. Billie would share the clip in response, and as Justin and his wife returned the love, the bond grew stronger.

The Coachella experience was about to be repeated in arenas and festivals across the globe as Billie set off on her When We All Fall Asleep World Tour. At the very first of these, at the Sparks Arena in Auckland, New Zealand, Billie and Finneas sat on the front of the stage and delivered the first live performance of "i love you," an acoustic stripped-back version. The crowd stopped singing and screaming—for a minute—and just soaked it in.

With her friend Denzel Curry or (occasionally) Finneas opening, the show moved to Australia, where Billie played to thousands in arenas in big cities and at Groovin the Moo festival venues all around the country. She returned in May and June to tour North America, playing venues five times bigger than she had ever played before.

She was known to throw the photographers out of the stage pit so that fans could get closer and mosh.

But whether she was performing at massive venues such as the sixteen-thousand-capacity Budweiser Stage in Toronto, the classy Metropolitan Opera House in Philadelphia, or outdoor venues like the Red Rocks Amphitheatre in Colorado, she had the ability to create an intimate relationship with her audience. She was known to throw the photographers out of the stage pit so that fans could get closer and mosh. She would involve fans in the songs, telling them to crouch down during the bridge of "COPYCAT" ("Lower, lower, lower," she'd cry) and leap up in a frenzy, imploring them to put down their phones and feel the moment in a ballad or even get them to hold hands and say "I love you" to one another.

It really felt like the summer of Billie. She was on the radio, constantly interviewed online, and on the cover of so many magazines. She appeared on the cover of *Billboard* in the US, *Vogue* in Australia, the *Sunday Times Magazine* in the UK, *Rockin'On* in Japan, *Glamour* in the Netherlands, *Elle Girl* in Russia, and many others, always looking elegant, fabulously styled, and interesting. For Billie, *Nylon Germany*, however, went too far. Its futuristic cover portrayed her as bald, with shiny metallic skin like a robot, and Billie responded angrily to the use of the fake photo, particularly as it made her—still a minor—appear as though she wasn't wearing a shirt.

She had also spoken out on her body image in an ad for Calvin Klein in May 2019. The thirty-second ad, "Billie Eilish speaks her truth," finds a green-tracksuited Billie in the bathroom. As she looks closely in the mirror (kissing her reflection) and lying fully clothed in the empty bath, she declares, "I never want the world to know everything about me." She goes on to explain: "That's why I wear big, baggy clothes. Nobody can be like, 'She's slim-thick,' 'She's not slim-thick,' 'She's got a flat ass,' 'She's got a fat ass.' No one can say any of that because they don't know."

At the same time, Billie appeared in a video for the American Ad Council's campaign "Seize the Awkward," which was designed to encourage young people to speak to friends about their mental health. Billie talks eloquently about anxiety and depression. She asks people to look out for their friends, check they are okay, and help, even just by giving them a hug. "I have seen it and I have been it," she says, talking from personal experience about how reaching out to someone can make a difference.

Billie talks eloquently about anxiety and depression. She asks people to look out for their friends, check they are okay, and help, even just by giving them a hug.

Just as Coachella had underestimated Billie's popularity, in the UK the iconic Glastonbury Festival had booked her for their Other Stage, the smaller sibling of the famous Pyramid Stage. However, the organizers had the good sense to move her up the bill, as forty thousand excited festival-goers packed the surrounding fields and matched the numbers attending the concurrent Miley Cyrus show at the Pyramid Stage.

With the BBC broadcasting the concert live on TV, this was a chance for young fans to catch Billie in action and for parents and casual viewers to see what the fuss was all about. Despite some technical issues (which she said was the reason for her angry face), she didn't disappoint and she threw herself into a memorable show. She made an immediate impression as she took to the stage in a Stella McCartney-designed T-shirt-and-shorts ensemble emblazoned with cartoons, including the Beatles's *Yellow Submarine* Blue Meanie characters, and complete with a bandana, white sunglasses, a surgical mask, and black muscle-support tape. She proceeded to rock the assembled masses with the same spirit she had shown all summer and completely stole the show in the English countryside, just as she had done in the Californian desert.

In the middle of the set, she recalled her first headlining show in London, when she had performed for two hundred people, and how amazing that felt, before adding, "It's like the whole world is looking at me right now." She wasn't wrong. It had been some summer.

CHAPTER FOURTEEN
FINNEAS

At the end of September 2019, a two-week gap appeared in the packed *When We All Fall Asleep, Where Do We Go?* schedule.

Billie and her team had played at every major festival across Europe and were due a break. One member of the team, who had perhaps worked harder than any of them, had other plans. Billie's brother, Finneas, picked this moment to release his first solo EP, which was called *Blood Harmony*.

Finneas had always been prepared to let the spotlight fall on Billie. Dedicated fans knew of the massive input he had on the songwriting and sound and recognized his spot-on harmonizing, but the massive success of *When We All Fall Asleep, Where Do We Go?* had brought Billie's self-effacing brother to the fore. And it was high time.

Standing six feet tall, with short, light brown hair (with a reddish tinge, like his mother's), the same piercing gray-blue eyes as his sister, and a well-groomed beard and moustache, Finneas cuts a handsome figure in his designer suits. Just like his sister, Finneas is likable, funny, and articulate in interviews.

The sensible older sibling, he uses fewer swear words and less teen slang than she does but expresses similar ideas about the power and freedom of creativity.

Finneas had, of course, grown up with music. He, too, was swept along by the family Beatles sing-alongs, his mom's songwriting classes, and his dad's mixtapes. He taught himself the piano and guitar, as well as spent time singing with the Los Angeles Children's Choir. In an interview with Ones to Watch, he said, in a characteristically witty and humble way, "I asked my dad how to play a Jon McLaughlin song so I could impress a girl. It didn't work . . . and instead I fell in love with music."

> **Songwriting was the same creative outlet and pleasure for Finneas as it was for Billie.**

By the time he was eleven, Finneas's passion had been sparked by the band Green Day. He described seeing them, in what was his first-ever concert, as a life-changing moment. Inspired by them and other guitar bands like My Chemical Romance and the Strokes, he formed his own bands with friends. Who knows where the Slightlys might be now if "ocean eyes" had never taken off?

Songwriting was the same creative outlet and pleasure for Finneas as it was for Billie. He claims to have written more than two hundred songs before "ocean eyes" (and swears they will never see the light of day!). As Billie's career took off, sweeping Finneas along as her cowriter, he never stopped writing his own songs. When he wrote with his sister, they were Billie Eilish songs—dark and quirky, following her vision and using her language and ideas. His own were more conventional singer-songwriter compositions. They were emotional love songs built around a traditional verse-chorus structure with the guitar or piano figuring prominently.

In August 2016, nine months after "ocean eyes" had first appeared and just days before Billie signed her record contract, her brother released his first single, "New Girl," just using the name Finneas. It was a seductive pop song with his velvety vocals combining with clever lyrics and a jaunty melody. It was well received by Billie's early fans and new-music blogs, but Finneas wasn't seeking stardom—he just wanted to put his music out there.

Fast-forward a year and, at Billie's first appearance in New Zealand, she stepped aside midshow to introduce Finneas. He played his soon-to-be released second single, the tender ballad "I'm in Love Without You." This midshow acoustic cameo would continue through Billie's 2017 and 2018 tours, during which time Finneas had released a string of singles, each one written, performed, and sung by him—even the backing vocals, which were sometimes choral.

They revealed how deft a songwriter he was and what a lush voice he possessed. He wrote and sang from the heart. His songs differed from those he cowrote with Billie in that his were straightforward lyrics about romance, love, and pain, albeit with wit and charm. Similarly, although the production was exquisite and crafted, it was less audacious or experimental.

What the songs did share was an authenticity and a willingness to cross genres. Some, like "Heaven," sung with a whispery voice to dark and echoing beats, or the catchy "Landmine," which employed staccato electronic pulses and layered vocal distortion, have that Highland Park bedroom feel. Others would present something very different, such as the piano-accompanied ballad "Break My Heart Again," the Frank Sinatra-esque crooning of

What the songs did share was an authenticity and a willingness to cross genres.

"Hollywood Forever," or the singer-songwriter-style "Life Goes On" and "Luck Pusher."

Whether writing from personal experience or from an understanding of the human heart, Finneas clearly had the ability to touch a nerve. "Break My Heart Again" was an unrequited-love song inspired by a series of text messages; "College" was a retort to bitter posts from an ex who had moved away; while "Let's Fall in Love for the Night" is a fantasy of the most romantic one-night stand ever.

As Finneas turned twenty-one in August 2018, these songs were getting noticed—combined Spotify and YouTube plays would be hundreds of thousands within the month. It's hypothetical to wonder whether his music would receive such attention without the connection to Billie, but some of those listening to Finneas made it clear he was their favorite O'Connell sibling.

Finneas had his own favorite fan . . . In October 2018, he had started a new relationship and it became very clear that he was head over heels in love. The girl he was dating was Claudia Sulewski, an incredibly popular social-media influencer who posted vlogs about beauty and fashion. She had around two million subscribers on YouTube and more than a million followers on Instagram.

After just a few months dating her, he had released a single titled "Claudia," a lively pop song set to a soft beat with earnest and self-conscious lyrics about her effect on him. Amazingly, it emerged he had written the first verse of the song and sent it to her on the day he met her. How's that for a romantic soul? Near the single's release date he revealed all this on Twitter and added: "When ya know, ya know." For her part, Claudia loved his sentimental gesture. She even provided the artwork for the single, an accomplished painting of an angel falling into a rose, which was animated for the video.

In 2019 Finneas began to play a few headline gigs in his own right. He was used to being onstage with Billie, but it was daunting to step out alone. He told the *NME* how fun and easy it was playing along with Billie and Andrew, but that this was something completely different: "I'm sweating, and wearing a suit, and tripping over myself," he told them. "It's super nerve-wracking."

Among his first solo headliners was a sold-out show at Baby's All Right, in Brooklyn, New York—coincidentally the first New York headliner his sister had played too. It wasn't that different. His appearances were greeted with screams and, initially to his surprise, the type of fan sing-alongs that he had grown accustomed to hearing at Billie Eilish shows. When it came to choosing a performer to open for Billie's 1 by 1 Tour, it must have been a no-brainer. They had a perfect warm-up act already on the bus.

Never having had the luxury of working in a fully equipped recording studio, Finneas had the advantage of being able to pack up his "studio" and take it on the road with him. Now that Billie had a full support team traveling with her, Finneas found he had time to devote to his own songs. He even said he got more done as he didn't have the distractions of home life. He would work in dressing rooms and hotel bedrooms in Berlin, Dublin, Texas, or Tokyo, sometimes walking straight offstage after a show to focus on a new song.

> **Now that Billie had a full support team traveling with her, Finneas found he had time to devote to his own songs.**

Finneas had worked on *Blood Harmony* at the height of the festival frenzy of summer 2019, releasing a few of the tracks as singles in the months before the October launch. It was a true indie production—released on Finneas's own OYOY label, distributed through AWAL, and available on vinyl too—and yet it was silkily produced, commercial, and wholeheartedly pop.

The tracks on *Blood Harmony* continue where his 2018 singles left off, with a focus on melody, Finneas's soulful voice, and the emotional punch of his lyrics. While synths, pulses, and effects are used, they are incidental rather than the mood-making orchestration of Billie's songs. Instead, we are treated to beautifully crafted guitar- and piano-based instrumentals backed by simple soft beats or handclaps.

Whether in ballads or his midtempo songs, it is Finneas's often anguished voice and his poetic, metaphor-laden lyrics that stand out. It was clear that Finneas often wrote from personal experience, both good and bad; and he talked of how he would distill his diary and events of his life into song. This is especially evident in the humility and emotional honesty of "I Lost a Friend," the painful denial of "I Don't Miss You at All," or the forensic examination of his infatuation in "Lost My Mind."

The most popular track on the EP was the exuberant, guitar-driven song "Shelter," which Finneas said he originally wrote for the mercurial Swedish DJ Avicii (who sadly died in 2018), simply because he liked the title. The video accompanying the song was a one-shot film of Finneas in a vest and a tie, striding along the dried-up Los Angeles riverbed (familiar to anyone who's seen the original *Grease* movie). He is joined by a horde of dancers in uniform blue joggers and turtlenecks whose choreography becomes aggressive as they turn on him, grabbing and shoving him around.

As the video clocked up a million views within a month of being uploaded, the *Blood Harmony* EP was also receiving critical acclaim and commercial success. It reached Number 11 in the *Billboard* Heatseekers chart for new acts, made the iTunes Top 50 in Brazil, Australia, Canada, and Spain, and the Top 100 in the UK, Germany, France, and Italy.

BLOOD HARMONY

The "blood harmony" theory suggests that some siblings have an innate ability to sing perfect harmonies with one another. Perhaps it is genetic, perhaps some kind of sixth sense. It is not a theory particularly supported by science, but pop-music history offers some strong evidence with the likes of the Louvin Brothers, the Carpenters, the Bee Gees, the Chicks, or First Aid Kit all proving the point. What is most likely is that siblings just have a chance to sing together from an early age and plenty of time to practice. This is certainly true of Finneas and Billie, who not only grew up in a family who loved singing but also, having the freedom that homeschooling facilitated, had more opportunities to sing together than most. Is "blood harmony" a real thing? Perhaps not, but it makes for a great album title!

Finneas was twenty-two, and he had truly come of age as an artist in his own right. Just a month after the release of his EP he left the family home and along with it his bedroom studio (although he reserved the right to go back there if he needed that certain ambience and sound!). He and Claudia had bought a house in Los Feliz by the Hollywood Hills in LA, just seven miles from Highland Park. Claudia even documented the move in a vlog. The large Spanish-style house had plenty of room for a new studio and, equally excitingly, for a new dog—a pit bull named Peaches.

The studio was essential. Finneas was now in demand as a producer and songwriter. Alongside the requests from Billie wannabes for him to produce them (which he politely declined), he also had some interesting invitations to work with various performers. As a producer he had learned from working with Billie. He had perfected the art of layering vocals, creating beats, or mixing real instruments and computer-created sounds. As a songwriter he now had an understanding of how to work with an artist, to get inside their mind, and create a song that they felt completely comfortable with.

At first, Finneas was content to work with upcoming artists such as Alice Kristiansen, R & B singer Evalyn, UK electro-pop trio Flawes, and Australian electronica singer Wafia. As his reputation grew, bigger names—Khalid, Tori Kelly, Sabrina Claudio, Ashe, and John Legend—came calling. His biggest coup came when his name appeared on the credits for Selena Gomez's massive global hit "Lose You to Love Me." Because he and Billie are on the same label as Selena, he was called in at the last minute to see if he could contribute anything to the song's production. According to Selena, he added the final touch that made all the difference to the track.

As a songwriter, he seemed to appeal to female singers. He says it is due to the vulnerability expressed in his lyrics being something that women were prepared to display more than men. Camila Cabello had turned to Finneas to help with a song on her 2019 album, *Romance*. He was already a big fan and found that, like Billie, Camila had her own visual ideas about what she wanted in her songs. For her part, Camila admired how he was moved by the details, the delicate moments of life. Together they wrote "Used to This" about how her friendship with Shawn Mendes turned into love.

Finneas was living the dream. He was collaborating with massive stars whose work he had always valued and was part of one of the most successful acts in the world. However, unlike Billie, he generally avoided many of the less attractive aspects of fame. He could walk around town or go to restaurants and only occasionally be recognized. He didn't need the heavy security that accompanied Billie everywhere. Then came the GRAMMYs . . .

At the 2020 show, the most prestigious in the world, Finneas took home five awards for his songwriting and production on "bad guy" and *When We All Fall Asleep, Where Do We Go?* Although he still had to play second fiddle to his sister, who also picked up five GRAMMYs, he was in every newspaper looking typically dapper on the red carpet in his Gucci suit. Remaining anonymous was going to be a lot harder from then on.

Through pure talent and hard work, Finneas had managed to reach the pinnacle of all aspects of his profession. His contribution to Billie's success had been fully recognized, his solo Blood Harmony Tour in late 2019 had sold out venues, and his production and songwriting skills were in demand from the great and good (with rumors that Shawn Mendes and James Blake were eager to team up). However, in his acceptance speech at *Variety*'s Hitmakers brunch in December 2019, Finneas addressed all this in one sentence. Standing next to Billie, he said, "There's been a lot of articles now about me being more than just Billie Eilish's brother, but just being Billie Eilish's brother is all I ever want to be."

At the 2020 show, the most prestigious in the world, Finneas took home five awards for his songwriting and production on "bad guy" and *When We All Fall Asleep, Where Do We Go?*

FINNEAS

CHAPTER FIFTEEN

HAPPY NOW...

How do you celebrate a triumph like Summerfest? If you're Billie, you change your hair color!

A few days after wowing the world at the festival, Billie's Instagram posts revealed her dramatic new look. At first, she appeared to have a spot of bright green where her hair was parted, but as she lifted the top layer of chestnut-brown locks she revealed the neon-green roots coming down past her ears. She complemented this with green-tinged shades, a black-and-green bandana, and a luminous-green necklace. The future (for now at least) was green!

An all-conquering hero, Billie returned home to LA to play back-to-back dates at the Shrine Expo Hall, where in 2015 she had witnessed her first-ever concert. During the show, she pointed to the very spot near the back where she and Finneas had watched the Neighbourhood. But there was no doubting who the fans there had come to see. Word had spread fast and green hair, hoodies, and beanies were everywhere—including the merch stand, where fans excitedly lined up for the Blohsh hoodies and T-shirts. For her part, Billie looked fabulous, tying her hair back to reveal the full glory of the green and adding unmissable long, sharp, clawlike, matching green fingernails.

She tore down the house— as she would night after night when the When We All Fall Asleep World Tour set off again in August. Fans in Austria, the Czech Republic, Moscow, Saint Petersburg, and Ireland, many of whom had followed

Billie looked fabulous, tying her hair back to reveal the full glory of the green and adding unmissable long, sharp, clawlike, matching green fingernails.

Billie since the start, were now given a chance to witness her perform live as the tour took her to new cities and countries. It had reached Spain in early September, when she posted the question, "Haven't you been waiting long enough?" and encouraged fans in New York to go and watch the famous Times Square screens at four in the afternoon.

The screens teased the video for "all the good girls go to hell," which appeared on YouTube the following day. Director Rich Lee, who had previously distinguished himself with videos for Eminem, Maroon 5, and Lana Del Rey, created a suitably apocalyptic scenario that picked up from the scene in the "bury a friend" video where multiple syringes were plunged into Billie's back. Here, the injections stimulate the growth of a huge pair of wings, with Billie playing the part of a fallen angel. The video, which is dominated by darkness and fire, sees Billie fall into an oily pit and, with tar-bound and burning wings, struggle through a flaming town. Save for silhouetted figures dancing amid the flames, she is all alone.

The video made the song's climate-change allusions explicit— and if it still wasn't clear to those helping the video rack up thirteen million views in the first twenty-four hours, Billie's accompanying note rammed the point home. "Our earth is warming up at an unprecedented rate, icecaps are melting, our oceans are rising, our wildlife is being poisoned, and our forests are burning," she wrote, before urging people to join the demonstrations later that month during the UN's Climate Action Summit.

Around this time, Billie gave an in-depth interview to *Elle* magazine. Inevitably, the conversation got around to Billie's depression. After describing the torrid time she had endured with her mental health over the past few years, she revealed that she was finally feeling better. She explained that it was not related to her success, but somehow connected to growing up and a change in the people around her. She used her own story to generate a positive message: "All I can say now is, for anybody who isn't doing well, it will get better. Have hope."

Having read this, it is easy to see a change in Billie in the TV interviews she gave in September 2019. While she had always been a great interviewee, thoughtful in her answers, and happy to talk on virtually any subject, here she seemed relaxed and her playful, humorous side emerged even more. This was evident at the GRAMMY Museum, where she and Finneas performed a short, laid-back set before being interviewed in front of the small audience. It was even clearer on show in her appearance on *The Tonight Show Starring Jimmy Fallon*. Despite wearing one surgical boot and having a sprain in her other foot, she smiled and laughed her way through the interview and a game of true confessions with Jimmy and stand-up comedian Colin Quinn. Billie's "confession" involved "farting in a friend's mouth" and making her throw-up—and incredibly it turned out to be true!

> **She used her own story to generate a positive message: "All I can say now is, for anybody who isn't doing well, it will get better. Have hope."**

After twenty seconds, however, the fun started as she began walking up the walls and dancing while horizontal. This was a live show; no one expected that.

The very next day Billie made her first appearance on the renowned *Saturday Night Live* (*SNL*), the biggest of all late-night TV shows, which is regularly watched by over seven million viewers. As it was the first episode of a new season, she recorded a teaser with the show's host Woody Harrelson and other *SNL* cast members. The ninety-second clip cast Billie as a new girl at school and a skateboard-toting Woody as the cool pupil offering to show her around. It raised a few laughs, mostly when regulars Colin Jost and Michael Che play bullying jocks who try, and fail, to knock Billie's book from her hand.

So much for the appetizer. The main course came on Saturday night as Billie took the stage to perform "bad guy." It all looked pretty normal as she appeared in a self-designed black shirt and shorts emblazoned with primary-colored, graffiti-style symbols, and started dancing and singing in a small one-room set. After twenty seconds, however, the fun started as she began walking up the walls and dancing while horizontal. This was a live show; no one had expected that. Or that the fun would continue as she walked across the ceiling and danced upside down.

It was a real water-cooler moment and one that Billie herself described as a "peak life experience." Billie later explained that it was inspired by a 1951 movie called *Royal Wedding*, where Fred Astaire pulled off the same trick. It involved the camera being attached to the set, which was rotated through 360 degrees. Billie worked out the choreography using her two fingers in a shoebox and figured that as long as she stayed focused, knew where she was at every moment, and ignored the pain from her two badly sprained ankles and the exhaustion from hours of rehearsal, she'd be OK.

Later in the show, Billie and Finneas returned to perform "i love you." If proof was needed of Billie's versatility and talent here it was, as she sang a song with a completely different vibe. In front of a star-filled background, wearing identical Gucci brown-patterned his-and-her suits, they delivered a beautiful live version, with Finneas providing the most perfectly judged harmonies.

THE *VANITY FAIR* INTERVIEWS

On October 18, 2019, Billie Eilish sat down with *Vanity Fair* to respond to the same questions she had answered on the same date as a fifteen-year-old in 2017 and as a sixteen-year-old in 2018. Each video was shared on YouTube, with Billie commenting on the previous interviews in her responses. Each year, she believes she is about as successful as she could ever be—and yet her answers are testament to her meteoric rise. She reveals the number of Instagram followers she has (which grows from 257,000 to over 40 million!) and the most famous contact on her phone (from Khalid to Drake), while 2019 Billie just laughs at her 2018 self when she says she could probably go to the local grocery store, Trader Joe's, without being recognized.

In many ways she's the same Billie: speaking from the heart, articulate and sassy but sensitive. She is always willing to call out her younger self for being naive, for saying that all artists are sad, for going to ridiculous levels to avoid swearing, for being conceited for wanting to write a song no one has ever heard ("What an idiot!"), or even for just being cute—"Look at that nose," she says. "Like a little button!"

Some of the more revealing answers concern her attitudes to fame. She changes from initially being excited about her fame to finding it difficult to deal with it, to accepting it for what it is. "I like being famous," she says in 2019. "It's very weird, but it's very cool." In the last of the interviews she is also able to open up on her changing mental health—how her drop in confidence in 2018 reflected the mood she was in at the time and the importance she places on maintaining her current happiness.

Some parts of the interviews remain comfortingly unwavering. She doesn't have a boyfriend (although in 2019 she admits she actually was seeing someone when questioned in 2018), she should never relay everything she thinks on social media, *Fruitvale Station* is her favorite movie, Finneas is always her best friend, and when her mom appears at the end to give her a hug, it is always a tearjerker.

Billie has never shied away from supporting campaigns and causes that she believes in. She had launched Billie's Closet, selling her personal clothing to raise funds for the Pawsitive Change Prison Program, which matches shelter dogs with prison inmates;

she has spoken out against anti-abortion laws and supported reproductive-health advocates Planned Parenthood. She has also invited HeadCount, a group campaigning to get young people to register to vote, to every single date on her US tour.

As a chart-topping artist, Billie was receiving requests to help all kinds of charities. One of the most high-profile invitations she accepted was for the annual We Can Survive concert at the Hollywood Bowl in Los Angeles to raise money for cancer research. A crowd of nearly eighteen thousand were in attendance for an all-star cast that included Lizzo, the Jonas Brothers, Taylor Swift, Camila Cabello, Marshmello, Becky G, and Halsey. It was, however, Billie, resplendent in an all-green outfit, who was the most enthusiastically greeted and her miniset really got the Bowl rocking.

A week later, on October 27, she was performing at a more intimate event but for a cause that was just as important. The Annual UNICEF Masquerade Ball is promoted by UNICEF Next Generation, part of the organization that focuses on young adults striving to improve the lives of children, and Billie was the perfect guest. Photos of her posing at the Halloween event set the internet alight as she stood wearing an all-black outfit consisting of a Playboy Sad Bunny hoodie, a demonic-skull

Some said it was punk, and some claimed it was goth, but it was pure Billie.

T-shirt, and zip-embellished pants, with a crystal face mask and spiky shoes adding to the scary effect. Some said it was punk, and some claimed it was goth, but it was pure Billie.

It was no secret that Billie and Finneas had been working on new material before and since the album's release. They had become comfortable with recording in hotel rooms while touring, and Finneas had talked of how they had songs "percolating." It did put pressure on them, though, and Billie responded to desperate fans' questions in early November on Instagram, saying, "Yes, I have two unreleased songs that are coming that you haven't heard any of . . . Be patient, damn!"

Every note and word of the song is so deliberate and considered.

On November 13, 2019, the first of these dropped. Titled "everything i wanted," it is connected to the album by its first line, which cites a nightmare in which Billie kills herself by jumping off the Golden Gate Bridge in San Francisco and discovers that no one really cares. Billie and Finneas had even called the song "Nightmare" when they began working on it a year earlier. It's a song that's loaded with meaning, and reflects on fame, self-esteem, expectations, fulfillment, and love.

The instrumental track drives the song with a brisk but soft padded beat interspersed with piano parts, handclapping, and synth chords. It teeters on the edge of melancholia, but an uplifting melody always saves it. Billie's vocals transition from breathy intonation to sweet singing, with carefully placed echoes to the ends of her lines adding depth and emotion. For the first time ever (as Billie notes in a "making of" video) there is an outro to one of her songs. What is clear is that Billie and Finneas really apply themselves to the process of songwriting, and every note and word of the song is so deliberate and considered.

Billie had talked about fame before. Anyone who had risen so quickly in the public eye would find it difficult. She had said that media intrusions, the impossibility of going out without being mobbed, and online criticism were difficult to live with, but that she consoled herself with the connection with fans and the buzz of live shows. "Everything i wanted" dealt head-on with the idea of fame not being everything it seemed, and with the complications and contradictions it presents. This was balanced with the chorus, which celebrates her relationship with Finneas, whose love and care is permanent and unchanging. He remains her anchor as she negotiates the stormy waters of fame.

"Everything i wanted" entered the Top 10 all around the world (reaching Number 8 in the US, Number 3 in the UK, and Number 1 in Ireland, Norway, and the Baltic states of Lithuania, Estonia, and Latvia). It was also made available (in the US) as a flexi disc, a superthin vinyl record. Billie's EP and album had been released in vinyl format (and on cassette tape too), and her next release would appear only in the retro format.

Billie traveled to Third Man Records in Nashville, owned by Jack White, to perform an acoustic set in front of 250 family and friends. She and Finneas played a forty-minute set that was immediately put on to acetate for a vinyl pressing. "Do you see that?" Billie reportedly said, pointing out the white-coated technicians in the adjacent glass-fronted booth. "They're like making my voice onto a thing. Like right now! That's crazy." There was no official video of the show (in which Billie wore rock-and-roll black leather pants), but there was one of Billie in yellow fisherman's hat, personally splatter painting the record sleeves of the limited-edition release.

November was also to bring the novel experience of the awards season—and Billie was expected to be among the leading contenders. She had received an incredible six nominations for each of the two big ceremonies: the American Music Awards (AMAs) and the GRAMMYs. While the latter was the most prestigious, many artists favor the AMAs, especially because their awards are decided through fan votes.

> **She had received an incredible six nominations for each of the two big ceremonies: the American Music Awards (AMAs) and the GRAMMYs.**

The 2019 AMAs, broadcast live across the US on November 24, was Billie's first-ever awards show. She began by owning the red carpet as she posed in head-to-toe retro Burberry plaid, including a custom-made white bonnet with a glittery mesh veil (which some compared to a beekeeper's headgear). In this outfit—without the hat, but sucking a lollipop and visibly shaking—she picked up her first-ever award, for Alternative Artist.

In all her vivid dreams, Billie could never have conceived of a year like 2019.

She then hit the stage. The Microsoft Theater in LA was turned into a hellish, flame-filled room as she belted out "all the good girls go to hell," and she even approached the camera to sing right into the living rooms of America. She was rocking the black T-shirt with red jewels that spelled out No Music on a Dead Planet (the slogan of the Music Declares Emergency climate-change awareness campaign) when she collected her second award, for New Artist of the Year.

At the AMAs Billie had introduced the band Green Day, saying that "growing up, there was no band more important to me or my brother." A few days earlier, *Rolling Stone* magazine had got her together with the band's singer, Billie Joe Armstrong, and it was incredible how much the two artists, from different generations and with totally different audiences, had in common. Billie Joe especially admired Billie's music for being "earnest" and sounding like "freedom," but if he passed on one lesson from his own experience, it was that she should stop and appreciate the moment as "the feeling of when you first get popular as a musician, that never happens twice."

This was that moment. In all her wildest dreams, Billie could never have conceived of a year like 2019. In just twelve months she played at Coachella and Glastonbury and to massive sold-out crowds around the world, posed for iconic magazine cover shoots, recorded a Number 1 single and the biggest-selling album of the year, impressed with TV appearances, won major awards, and heard uber celebrities from Elton John to Dave Grohl and from Julia Roberts to Shawn Mendes declare their love for her. However, in her last *Vanity Fair* interview Billie had defined success not as how many people *knew* you, but how people *felt* about you. Even as she said it, she knew she was now loved by millions, who saw her as an inspiration. She was a phenomenal success.

HAPPY NOW ...

CHAPTER SIXTEEN

GRAMMYS, OSCARS, AND JAMES BOND

When I first heard Billie sing, I kinda stopped breathing for a sec.

It was so emotional and so deep—it stopped me . . . I think you're magical—and this is just the beginning." Many around the world had had similar thoughts over the past few years, but it was groundbreaking singer-songwriter Cyndi Lauper who found the words as she presented Billie with the *Billboard* 2019 Woman of the Year Award in December 2019.

Billie was receiving praise from many of the artists she had looked up to all her life. Alicia Keys was another of them. Billie was a guest when she hosted *The Late Late Show,* and it became a mutual-appreciation session. For her part, Billie enthused over a cover of "ocean eyes" Alicia had posted on Instagram and then showed a clip of her as a twelve-year-old singing the Alicia Keys hit "Fallin'" at a talent show. To cap it all they then performed "ocean eyes" as a duet with Alicia at the piano.

Amidst the awards shows, parties, and interviews, Billie was due to celebrate her eighteenth birthday at the end of that month, but she still managed to achieve another landmark before reaching adulthood: she directed her first official video. With a love of film-making, Billie had been pushing to direct her videos since the very beginning, but only with the release of the video for "xanny" had she been trusted to call the shots behind the camera.

The video, a single shot with no edits, shows Billie sitting on a white bench in a white-tiled room. She wears a cream turtleneck sweater and ski pants; her hair is a natural brown and it's matched by her long fingernails. Her art as director is to captivate the viewer for the four and a half minutes of the video through the movement of the camera, her own listless and tortured performance and the shock factor as arms emerge from off-camera to push cigarette butts into her face. That it was an assured directorial debut was confirmed by the ten million views it earned over twenty-four hours.

Her art as director is to captivate the viewer for the four and a half minutes of the video.

That said, Billie could give an engrossing performance strapped into the passenger seat of a car. She'd done just that in her appearance in "Carpool Karaoke," a feature of *The Late Late Show with James Corden* where a guest is driven around by the affable host as they both join in, singing to their (or sometimes others') hits on the car stereo. Some forty-five million people have seen the fifteen-minute clip on YouTube, in which the pair enjoy a sing-along. Billie also gets out her ukulele in the car and plays songs from her childhood. They also visit her family home. There, James Corden gets to sit in the room where they made the album (the filled-in whiteboard track list still on the wall), and to see for himself how close Billie and her mom are, and to be freaked out by Billie's pet spider (a blue tarantula who had sadly died by the end of the year).

Only close friends were invited to Billie's eighteenth birthday party, where, like so many others, she danced, smashed a piñata, and blew the candles out on her cake, a vegan chocolate cake with vegan cream cheese frosting and peppermint candies, baked, at Billie's request, by her mother. Billie didn't forget her fans, though. They received their own present in the form of a previously unseen video of a four-year-old Billie cleverly intercut with clips of her performing to thousands.

Billie said the best thing about being eighteen was that (in California) she could now drive after 11 p.m. This was possibly the inspiration behind the video for "everything i wanted," which was uploaded on January 23 and was the second video she had directed. This was more ambitious, as it followed Billie driving Finneas through the city to the coast and into the ocean. The siblings seem disengaged and lost in their own worlds until the car begins to sink to the seabed. Only then do they exchange a glance and a smile as they join hands. It is so dark and disturbing, and yet there is a warmth that shines through and echoes the video's opening statement: that Billie and her brother will always be there for each other.

When Billie appeared on *Jimmy Kimmel Live!* she made it clear which event she was most looking forward to. "As cool as everything else is," she said, "it's the GRAMMYs. I've watched that every single year of my entire life; like, judging all the girls' ugly-ass dresses." She had been nominated for six awards, but winning them was a different matter. After all, Lil Nas X also had six nominations, while Lizzo trumped them all with eight nods. Then there were Ariana Grande, Lewis Capaldi, Taylor Swift, and Lana Del Rey—great artists, all with a chance of winning a coveted gilded gramophone.

It is so dark and disturbing, and yet there is a warmth that shines through and echoes the video's opening statement: that Billie and her brother will always be there for each other.

The 62nd Annual GRAMMY Awards took place at the Staples Center in LA on January 26, 2020, in the shadow of the news of the tragic death that morning of Kobe Bryant, a basketball star who had played for the Los Angeles Lakers at that very arena. Many people paid tribute to Bryant, but the excitement and glitz of the show overcame the sadness that many felt. By the time Billie and Finneas arrived on the red carpet, the TV cameras and paparazzi were out in force. Billie's outfit would be as talked about as the awards; in fact, so much so that the *New York Times* declared, "She had already won the night." She did look like a million dollars in a green-and-black Gucci suit layered over a long-sleeved, sequinned turtleneck. Even her nails carried a Gucci label in two shades of green. Gold Gucci earrings featuring a gold lion head, a Blohsh silver pendant, and fingerless gloves completed the breathtaking ensemble. Finneas wasn't too scruffy either as he walked the carpet in a floral Gucci smoking jacket with a floppy bow tie and buckle boots.

Billie and Finneas were among the stars to perform at the ceremony. Wearing matching cream suits (Gucci again!) they silenced the massive arena with an emotional rendition of "when the party's over." It was celebrated by many critics as the best performance of the evening, but of course, Billie and Finneas were not just there to perform. It turned out to be a night to remember as they each took home five awards—Billie becoming only the second artist ever to win all of the "big four" categories: Best New Artist, Album of the Year, Song of the Year, and Record of the Year.

It turned out to be a night to remember as they each took home five awards.

The trophy-laden siblings even admitted that they were embarrassed to have won so many. "So many other songs deserve this, I'm sorry," Billie said in her acceptance speech for Song of the Year. Then, as the Album of the Year was announced—what would be her fifth win of the night—she was spotted mouthing the words, "Please don't be me." After accepting that award, she said *Thank U, Next* "deserved" to have won, adding that Ariana Grande's album had helped her during some difficult times. Finneas, too, was humble in an evening that confirmed him as one of the world's top producers

Finneas dedicated one of his wins to "all the kids who make music in their bedrooms."

and songwriters, and he dedicated one of his wins to "all the kids who make music in their bedrooms."

There is really only one award ceremony that is bigger than the GRAMMYs, and that's the world-famous Academy Awards, commonly known as the Oscars. And guess where Billie was going next? For the red carpet, she ditched the Gucci for Chanel, wearing a cream-colored jacket-and-pants ensemble, pinned with diamond-studded Chanel logos and paired with "Cha" and "nel" fingerless gloves that drew attention to her long, black, jeweled fingernails. Fellow fashion outlier actor Billy Porter stopped her on the red carpet to ask about her favorite movies when she was growing up. "*Babadook*," she replied, causing many to Google to check she meant the 2014 version. Well, she was only twelve when it came out!

This time, she wasn't up for any awards, but accompanied on piano by Finneas she sang a poignant cover of the Beatles's "Yesterday" as the Academy ran its "In Memoriam" tribute to luminaries who had died in 2019. Though many loved their version of the classic, Billie wasn't one of them. She labeled it "trash" and said she "bombed." She clearly didn't enjoy the evening, saying that she wasn't feeling well and that, in contrast to the GRAMMYs, she felt out of place among all the movie stars.

She said she felt terrified and, unusually for her, was racked with nerves when called to perform.

A week or so later, at the Brits—the British version of the GRAMMYs—she was back among her own people. Billie was all smiles when she went up to collect the award for Best International Female Artist from Spice Girl Melanie C and laughed with Lizzo, who was yelling, "I love you!" from the audience. But she became emotional during her acceptance speech, explaining that she had been feeling hated recently (she was referring to vitriolic online posts about her), but said that the warmth of the audience had brought her to tears.

BILLIE ONLINE

When Billie was born, there was no Facebook, Twitter, or Instagram. By the time she was thirteen, no self-respecting teenager would be without an account on one or all of them, and she was no exception. She loved posting pictures of herself, making new friends, and relaying her feelings. Even before she was famous, she had hundreds of followers.

As her career took off, Twitter became an important channel for communicating with fans. Until it became impossible, she would try to respond to anyone who contacted her. She held little back, revealing her moods and her thoughts. Fans lapped up relatable posts like "stop being so cute sheesh im tryna get over u" or "command z my whole life." Unfortunately,

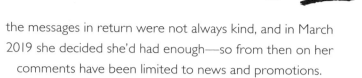

the messages in return were not always kind, and in March 2019 she decided she'd had enough—so from then on her comments have been limited to news and promotions.

Instagram was a similar story. She recalled having various Instagram usernames, including @rideroftwind, @dead.cow, and @disasterpiece, but by the time "ocean eyes" was out she had settled on the slightly random @wherearetheavocados (a phrase she once screamed when making some grilled cheese) and limited herself to following 666 people, saying she wasn't a Satanist, she just liked the number!

Fans were united in their love of @wherearetheavocados, devouring the daily photos that documented the development of her style from normal teen wear to baggy hip-hop to Chanel and Gucci designer outfits. Some even adopted an unofficial fandom name of "Avocados." However, in May 2019 Billie deleted the account and along with it every post. An @billieeilish account replaced it, but for many fans it would never be the same.

Billie now says that if she could tell her younger self one thing, it would be not to post online so often. In February 2020 she told the BBC that she had stopped reading the comments on posts as it was "ruining her life." It was a sad conclusion for someone who had firmly believed in communicating with her fans.

The hurtful trolling was one more burden of the massive public profile that Billie had gained. Her triumph at the GRAMMYs was one thing, and the Oscars another, but Billie and Finneas had just released the theme tune to the new James Bond movie—the latest installment in one of the biggest film franchises in the world. It had been something they had long dreamed of doing, and they had made it clear to their team that they would jump at the chance. When they met Bond producer Barbara Broccoli at their show in Ireland in August 2019, it became one more ambition that they could make happen. Broccoli sent them the script for the opening scene of the new movie, *No Time to Die*, and it was up to Finneas and Billie to create something that she and James Bond himself, Daniel Craig, would love.

That was the tricky part. With a couple of days free while on tour, Billie and Finneas had hired a studio to work on a song. Nearly every artist records their music in a studio with state-of-the-art production equipment, but there is something about this setup that inhibits Billie and Finneas. They struggled to come up with anything. Only later, on a tour bus in Texas, did the idea for their "No Time to Die" take shape.

Billie reflected that consciously and subconsciously they had been trying to write Bond themes all their lives. This rings true as "No Time to Die" begins with the familiar minimalist synth, whisper singing and lyrics of lies and deceit perfectly matching the seductiveness, secrecy, and danger associated with the famous spy. Then they audaciously introduce elements new to their music. There are guitar chord progressions, discordant brass, an orchestra crescendo, and Billie belting out vocals like a diva. To cap all these hallmarks of Bond themes through the years, the song finishes, just like Monty Norman's original Bond theme, with a minor ninth chord. The song was a masterful creation, an original and unique homage to a fifty-year tradition.

Billie performed "No Time to Die" live for the first time at the

Billie reflected that consciously and subconsciously they had been trying to write Bond themes all their lives.

Brit Awards, accompanied not just by Finneas but also a full orchestra led by celebrated composer Hans Zimmer and former Smiths guitarist Johnny Marr. The single immediately became Billie's first Number 1 in the UK, as well as being only the second Bond theme ever to top the charts.

> **The single immediately became Billie's first Number 1 in the UK, as well as being only the second Bond theme ever to top the charts.**

The GRAMMYs recognized Billie's recording achievements, the Oscars confirmed she was one of the finest performers around, and the Bond theme placed her among the great icons of pop music. She was rapidly collecting all the monuments of popular culture. Another was on its way. In March 2020 Billie became the cover model for American *Vogue* magazine, the most famous fashion publication in the world.

Vogue produced three different print covers of Billie, with a headline proclaiming her as "The Outsider." Each cover shot was taken by a different leading photographer and features Billie sporting a different brand. Harley Weir took the Prada version, an intriguing close-up of Billie resting her face in her hands, her green hair and nails matching the Prada Linea Rossa jacket. The Hassan Hajjaj cover uses a portrait of Billie looking thoughtfully at the camera. Her black hair hangs down past her shoulders with the vivid green prominent, and she wears a striped Gucci jacket with a chunky chain of linked Gucci "G"s. The camera moves farther out for Ethan James Green's half-body shot of Billie looking strident in a jungle-print Versace parka. A fourth cover was available as a digital-only version. This featured a fabulous lifelike drawing of Billie in a Louis Vuitton "Exorcist" dress by Nastya Kovtun. Billie selected the sixteen-year-old Russian fan herself from drawings she had posted of her on Instagram.

To appear on a *Vogue* cover—in a unique style of her own—was an incredible achievement. Billie had always loved fashion. When she had no money, she would cut up clothes and sew parts of them together to form new outfits. She even posted a photo of herself wearing a shirt refashioned from an IKEA bag. As she became more famous, she collaborated with Bershka, Siberia Hills, and Freak City fashion brands to create new lines. Then, in January 2020, she launched a line of T-shirts, bucket hats, a fanny pack, and oversized sweatshirts available worldwide at H&M stores with every item in the collection made using sustainable materials.

Billie's environmental concerns were also at the fore when she announced her 2020 Where Do We Go? World Tour. She brought in the nonprofit organization Reverb to help foster an eco-conscious environment both backstage and in the arenas, with an ecovillage giving advice and resources stationed at every show. The forty-two-stop tour, featuring concerts at massive arenas across the US, Europe, and Latin America, sold out in hours. Those who were lucky enough to get tickets were in for a huge surprise. Before the opening show in Miami, a video played showing Billie taking off her shirt and then submerging herself in a pool of black liquid. In voiceover, she speaks out against both those who praise and who criticize her body. "You have opinions about my opinions, about my music, about my clothes, about my body," she says. "Some people hate what I wear, some people praise it. Some people use it to shame others, some people use it to shame me." In a powerful statement, Billie

When she had no money, she would cut up clothes and sew parts of them together to form new outfits. She even posted a photo of herself wearing a shirt refashioned from an IKEA bag.

admonishes the sexist treatment of her and other famous women and demands respect and recognition of her humanity.

Billie is now a massive star in every continent on the planet.

The video was expected to play before every concert in the tour. In early March, however, the global coronavirus pandemic forced the tour's postponement. Breaking the news, Billie said, "i'm so sad to do this but we need to postpone these dates to keep everyone safe. we'll let you know when they can be rescheduled. please keep yourselves healthy. i love you." Many of her tour dates have been tentatively rescheduled beginning in May 2021.

She has, however, promised she will be making new music in 2020 (how much will be released is less clear). Fans also still have an Apple TV+ film on Billie to savor. Acclaimed documentary maker R. J. Cutler has been filming since 2018, and for once, Billie has had little input. Understandably, she's a little freaked out by this. "Who has that much footage of them that they've never seen?" she told *NME*. "I'm terrified."

Billie has become a massive star in every continent on the planet, and her place in pop music history is already secured. Looking back on her journey to this point, it seems it could only ever have been undertaken by Billie—someone with her family support, with a sibling as talented as Finneas, with her boundless creativity, and with her don't-give-a-damn attitude. Without trying to do so, she has expressed the emotions, anxieties, and dreams of a generation and found millions who are eternally grateful that she has. Along with her brother, she has produced some of the freshest and most remarkable music around and has maintained an unrivaled close connection with her supporters. Billie has the world at her feet, and it's exciting to wonder what she will achieve in the future. She is capable of so much, but it's clear that whatever it is will be on her terms—and Billie's journey is far from over.

ACKNOWLEDGMENTS

The openness and honesty of Billie Eilish and Finneas O'Connell in interviews throughout their careers makes them the most refreshing and interesting of musicians, and has made this book so much easier to research. Closer to home, I am indebted to Becca Wright for her enthusiasm, suggestions, and invaluable editing, and her ever-helpful and encouraging colleagues at Michael O'Mara, particularly Louise Dixon. I would like to thank Jeremy Martin for his insightful contributions, and my family and friends, who were always willing to read drafts and discuss Billie's fascinating journey.

PICTURE CREDITS

Page 1: Araya Diaz / WireImage / Getty Images

Page 2: Steven Lovekin / Shutterstock (top); Invision / AP / Shutterstock (bottom)

Page 3: Nicholas Hunt / WireImage / Getty Images

Page 4: Frank Hoensch / Redferns / Getty Images (top); Amy Harris / Invision / AP / Shutterstock (bottom)

Page 5: Richard Polk / Getty Images for KROQ / Entercom

Page 6: Jeff Kravitz / FilmMagic / Getty Images (top); Rich Fury / Getty Images for Coachella (bottom)

Page 7: Jo Hale / Redferns / Getty Images (top); Roberto Finizio / NurPhoto via Getty Images (bottom)

Page 8: Jason Richardson / Alamy Live News

Page 9: Samir Hussein / WireImage / Getty Images

Page 10: Sara Jaye Weiss / Shutterstock

Page 11: Rebecca Sapp / WireImage for The Recording Academy / Getty Images (top); Jack Plunkett / invision / AP / Shutterstock (bottom)

Page 12: Chris Polk / Variety / Shutterstock (top); Chelsea Lauren / Shutterstock (bottom)

Page 13: David Swanson / EPA-EFE / Shutterstock (top); Rich Fury / Getty Images for iHeartMedia (bottom)

Page 14: JM Enternational / Shutterstock

Page 15: Kevin Winter / Getty Images (top); Rich Fury / VF20 / Getty Images for Vanity Fair (bottom)

Page 16: Kevin Mazur / Getty Images for Live Nation

INDEX

Academy Awards. *See* Oscars
Album of the Year (GRAMMYs), 204
Alternative Artist awards, 196
American Music Awards (AMAs), 195
Amsterdam, the Netherlands, 83, 99
Anderson, Tim, 54
Annie Mac, 117, 144, 146, 153
Apple Music, 38, 41, 54, 77, 111
Apple Store, 132
Apple TV, 211
Armstrong, Billie Joe, 196
Artists Without A Label (AWAL), 38
A$AP Rocky, 28, 93, 120
Astronomyy, 32, 50
Atlanta, GA, 82
Auckland, New Zealand, 18, 75, 94–95, 168
Aurora, 19, 31
Austin, TX, 53, 102, 104, 129, 151
Australia
  appears on Triple J, 95
  "bad guy," 164
  Blood Harmony, 180
  "bury a friend," 142
  dont smile at me, 69, 75
  first to take Billie to its heart, 89
  Florence and the Machine, 133, 138
  Laneway Festival, 92
  "lovely," 107
  "when the party's over," 131
  When We All Fall Asleep World Tour, 169
  "you should see me in a crown," 119
Austria, 107, 188

Babadook, 205
Baby's All Right, Brooklyn, NY, 179
"Bad" (Jackson), 95
Bad Teacher, 16, 25
Baird, Maggie, 14–17, 78, 91, 138
Baker, Alexandra, 52
Barcelona, Spain, 146
BBC, 53, 89, 117, 144, 170, 207
Beatles, the, 15, 129, 144, 171, 176, 205
Beats 1 radio show, 41, 105, 113, 168
Belgium, 143
Berlin, Germany, 83, 99, 143, 179
Best International Female Artists (Brits), 206

Best New Artist awards, 204
Best Super Short Horror Film Award (Shriekfest), 142
Bieber, Justin
  Billie's posters, 20, 56
  Blackbear and, 32
  in Billie's audience, 166
  "industry plants," 37
  principal entry for, 167–168
  Vanity Fair, 111
Big Fish Theory (Staples), 90
Billboard, 141
  Alternative Digital Song Sales Chart, 52
  Billie on cover, 169
  Heatseekers chart, 180
  Hot 100, 107, 142, 164
  200 chart, 7, 88, 106, 164
  Woman of the Year, 81, 201
Billie Eilish Experience, 159
Blackbear, 32, 49–50
Blah Blah Blah Science, 32
Blake, James, 183
Blohsh
  Coachella, 165
  fans and, 129, 187
  origins of, 125–126
  silver pendant, 204
  Takashi Murakami collaboration, 152
  Trevor Project donation, 145
Blood Harmony (Finneas), 175, 179–181, 183
BLU J, 50
"Body Count" (Reyez), 129
"Boyfriend" (Bieber), 32
Brazil, 74, 164, 180
"Break My Heart Again" (Finneas), 177–178
Brit Awards, 209
Broccoli, Barbara, 208
Brooklyn, NY, 131, 179
Brussels, Belgium, 99
Bubbling Under Hot 100 Chart, 52
Budweiser Stage, Toronto, Canada, 169
Bull, Devyck, 112
Burkhart, Samantha, 52

Cabello, Camila, 163, 182, 193
"Call Me Back" (The Strokes), 102

Calvin Klein, 120, 169
Cambridge, MA, 79
Canada, 69
  Blood Harmony, 180
  "bury a friend," 142
  first headline tour, 77
  "lovely," 107
  Toronto, 79
  "when the party's over," 131
  "you should see me in a crown," 119
career of Billie Eilish
  all four big awards, 80–81, 204–205
  Beats 1 radio show, 113
  Blohsh, 125–126
  breaking through, 37–38
  Coachella, 165–168
  dancing abilities, 18, 26, 29, 33, 112
  Darkroom, 43, 51
  discovers hip-hop, 28–29, 42
  EP, 61–62, 64–69, 73, 75, 87, 195
  fans, 69, 73, 75, 83, 101, 129
  festivals, 53–54, 168–170
  first awards show, 196
  Florence and the Machine, 133
  Groupies Have Feelings Too, 113
  injuries, 115–116
  James Bond theme, 208–209
  James Corden, 13, 77, 167, 202
  Justin Bieber, 167–168
  Khalid and, 105–107
  Netflix, 54
  1 by 1 Tour, 121, 126, 131, 142–147, 179
  online, 206–207
  Platoon, 38, 41, 51, 57
  Roma (film), 139
  "Snippet into Billie's Mind, A," 155
  spiders, love of, 118, 120, 126, 152, 202
  Takashi Murakami, 119, 152
  touring, 77–79
  trip to Asia, 119
  Tyler, the Creator and, 41–43
  ukulele playing, 15, 44, 68, 73–75,
    113, 129, 156, 202
  uploading to SoundCloud, 26–27, 30
  Vanity Fair interviews, 137, 191–192, 197
  Vogue covers, 169, 209–210
  We Can Survive concert, 193
  Where Do We Go? World Tour, 210
  Wheres My Mind Tour, 88, 93, 100,
    103, 120

"Carpool Karaoke" (Corden), 13, 15, 167,
    202
Cautious Clay, 32, 50
Central Presbyterian Church, 102
Chainsmokers, the, 39
Chanel, 131, 205, 207
Chaves, Michael, 142
Cheat Codes, 39
Che, Michael, 190
Cherry Bomb (Tyler, the Creator), 42
Chicago, IL, 79, 114
Childish Gambino, 28, 114, 129
Childish Major, 126
"Claudia" (Finneas), 178
Climate Action Summit (UN), 189
Coachella, 7, 165–168, 170, 196
Cohen, Taylor, 106
"College" (Finneas), 178
Cologne, Germany, 99
Corden, James, 13, 77, 167, 202
Coup De Main, 89–90
Courtyard Theatre, London, UK, 64
Cover Room, 102
Cragun, Reo, 100, 114
Crocodile, Seattle, WA, 78
CRSSD Festival, San Diego, CA, 53
Cuarón, Alfonso, 139
Curry, Denzel, 28, 169
Cutler, R. J., 211
Czech Republic, 188

Dahl, Trevor, 39
Damani Dada, 94
"Dancing on My Own" (Robyn), 74
Dangerous Woman Tour (Grande), 112
Darkroom, 43, 51, 57
Dash Radio, 49
Davey, Arron, 32
Decorated Youth magazine, 64
Denmark, 143
Detroit, MI, 114
Diamandis, Marina, 19
Diary of a Wimpy Kid (Freudenthal), 17
Diaz, Fred, 29–30, 49
Digital Journal, 53
DJ Keiro, 100
DJ Khaled, 87
Dog Eats Dog World (Raine), 141
Dont Smile at Me Tour, 100

Drake, 103
  Billie's favorite song, 28
  Damani Dada, 94
  "Hotline Bling," 75, 113
  joining the ranks of, 164
  phone contacts, 191
DSCVR Artists to Watch List (Vevo), 89
Dublin, Ireland, 179

Earl Sweatshirt, 28, 41
Elle Girl, 169
Elle magazine, 56, 189
Ellen DeGeneres Show, The, 120, 168
Entertainment Weekly, 56
Enwright, Michael, 32
"Eres Tú" (Mocedades), 74
Estonia, 131, 195
Everything, Everything, 66
Ex Cops, 92

Facebook, 32, 39, 57, 61, 73, 88, 206
Fader magazine, 131
"Fallin'" (Keys), 201
Favicchio, AJ, 52
Feigelson, Denzyl, 38
Fendi, 111
Fenn, Emmit, 88
Fike, Dominic, 28
First Aid Kit, 181
Florence and the Machine, 133, 138
Flower Boy (Tyler, the Creator), 42
Folk, Jerry, 50
Fonda Theatre, Hollywood, CA, 132–133
Forbes, 164
Forbes 30 Under 30 list, 137
Forbes, Aron, 54
Fox Theater, Oakland, CA, 127
France, 143, 180
Freak City, 210
Free Bike Valet, 32
Fruitvale Station (Coogler), 192

Gazzo, 50
Germany, 180
Glamour, 169
Glasgow, UK, 18
Glastonbury, UK, 64, 170, 196
Glee, 16, 25
Goblin (Tyler, the Creator), 42
Goldhouse, 39, 50
Goodbye & Good Riddance (Juice WRLD), 106

Governors Ball Music Festival, New York, 107
GRAMMY Museum, 189
GRAMMYs, 163, 203, 205
  AMAs and, 195
  Billie recognized, 207, 209
  Brits, 206
  Finneas at, 183
  wins all four big ones, 7, 80–81
Grande, Ariana, 81–82, 112, 163, 168, 203, 205
Great American Music Hall, San Francisco, CA, 99
Green Day, 15, 176, 196
Grohl, Dave, 197
Groovin the Moo, 169
Groupies Have Feelings Too (Beats 1), 113
Gucci, 102, 111, 183, 191, 204–205, 207, 209

Halsey, 19, 54, 193
H&M, 210
"Happiness Is a Warm Gun" (the Beatles), 15
Harper's Bazaar, 55
Harrelson, Woody, 190
Hazard, Gibson, 102–103
HeadCount, 193
"Heartbeat" (Childish Gambino), 28
"Heaven" (Finneas), 177
Heaven (London nightclub), 99
High as Hope tour (Florence and the Machine), 133
Highland Park, Los Angeles, CA, 13–14, 20, 40, 64, 177, 181
Hi Hat club, 40, 67
Hillard, Chad, 32
"Hill, The" (Irglová), 74
Hillydilly.com, 32
Hits Daily Double website, 43
Hollywood Boulevard, 132
Hollywood Bowl, 193
"Hollywood Forever" (Finneas), 178
"Hotline Bling" (Drake), 75, 113

"I Don't Miss You at All" (Finneas), 180
Igor (Tyler, the Creator), 42
"I Lost a Friend" (Finneas), 180
"I'm in Love Without You" (Finneas), 75, 177
Indiana, 104

Instagram, 32, 63, 66, 82–83, 111, 120, 128–129, 137–141, 187, 191, 206–207, 209
  Alicia Keys, 201
  Billie and her fans, 73, 194
  Billie on, 56–57
  Claudia Sulewski, 178
  "idontwannabeyouanymore," 65
  Madison Leinster, 106
  Tyler, the Creator, 43
  veganism, 103–104
  "when the party's over," 131
  "wish you were gay," 145
Interscope Records, 43, 50, 57
Ireland, 131, 188, 195, 208
Irglová, Markéta, 74
Italy, 116, 143, 180
iTunes, 38, 41
"I Will" (the Beatles), 15, 129

"James Bond" movies, 7, 208–209
Japan, 119, 142, 152, 164, 169
J. Cole, 28, 114
"Jealous" (Labrinth), 74
Jimmy Kimmel Live!, 152, 154, 203
John, Elton, 197
Jost, Colin, 190
Joyrich, 126
Juice WRLD, 106

Kardashian, Kim, 79
KCRW, 32
Kesselhaus, Berlin, Germany, 143
Keys, Alicia, 201
Khalid, 77, 105–107, 120, 133, 182, 191
King, Gayle, 91
Klein, Saul, 38
Kovtun, Nastya, 209
Kriss Kross Amsterdam, 39

LA Children's Chorus (LACC), 17
Lady Gaga, 39, 43, 82, 166
Lana Del Rey, 19, 31, 43, 53, 188, 203
"Landmine" (Finneas), 177
Laneway Festival, 92, 94–95
Låpsley, 29, 31–32
Late Late Show, 201
Late Late Show with James Corden, 77, 202
Late Night with Jimmy Fallon, 42
Latvia, 195
Lauper, Cyndi, 201
LA Weekly, 25

La Zona Rosa, 54
Lee, Rich, 188
Leikeli47, 28
Leinster, Madison, 106
"Let's Fall in Love for the Night" (Finneas), 178
LGBTQ community, 145
"Life Goes On" (Finneas), 178
Life Inside Out (D'Agnenica), 16
Lil Pump, 28
Lithuania, 195
Lizzo, 193, 203, 206
"Location" (Khalid), 105
Lollapalooza, Chicago, IL, 114, 115, 140
London, UK, 64, 83, 99, 117, 141, 144–145, 171
"Look at Me" (XXXTentacion), 127
López Estrada, Carlos, 129
Lorde, 20, 32
Los Angeles, CA, 159, 193
  Highland Park, 13
  riverbed, 180
  Slightlys in, 25
  Sofar Sounds, 44
  Tenants of the Trees, 45
Los Angeles Children's Choir, 176
Los Angeles Lakers, 204
Los Angeles Times, 19
Los Feliz, Los Angeles, CA, 181
"Lost a Friend" (Finneas), 180
Louis Vuitton, 116, 118, 209
Lowe, Zane, 41, 43, 77, 105
Lubliner, Justin, 43
Luc Junior Tam, 112
"Luck Pusher" (Finneas), 178

Mahogany Sessions (YouTube), 87
Maida Vale Studios, London, UK, 144
Malaysia, 142
Malibu, CA, 45
Manchester, UK, 116
Marian Hill, 57, 92
Marquis, Brian, 78, 114
Marr, Johnny, 209
Mars, Bruno, 166
Marshall, Andrew, 92–93, 100, 102, 118, 131, 144, 152, 179
Martinez, Melanie, 19
McCartney, Stella, 57, 171
Melanie C, 206
Melbourne, Australia, 75, 80

Mendes, Shawn, 163, 182–183, 197
Mendler, Bridgit, 54
Metro, 115
Metropolitan Opera House, Philadelphia, 169
Mexico, 74
Meyers, Dave, 163
Miami, FL, 104, 210
Michl, 44
Microsoft Theater, Los Angeles, CA, 196
Milan, Italy, 99
Milano Rocks, 116
Miles and AJ, 52
Misha, 15
Montreal, Canada, 113–114, 129
Mo Pop, Detroit, MI, 114, 116–118
Moretz, Chloë Grace, 54
Mosaert, 112
Moscow, Russia, 188
Moses, 28
"Motto, The" (Drake), 28
MTV, 87
MTV News, 157
Mt. Wolf, 40
Mu, 45
Murakami, Takashi, 119, 152
Music Declares Emergency (climate
    change awareness), 196
Music Inspired by the Film Roma, 139
music of Billie Eilish
    "!!!!!!," 154, 156
    "6.18.18," 127
    "8," 74, 154, 156
    "all the good girls go to hell," 155,
        165–166, 188, 196
    "bad guy," 154–155, 158–159,
        163–165, 168, 183, 190
    "bellyache," 44, 50–53, 57, 64, 68, 77,
        80, 88, 93, 95, 126, 129, 131
    "bitches broken hearts," 88, 104
    "Bored," 54, 62
    "bury a friend," 28, 140–143, 152–154,
        156, 166, 188
    "come out and play," 132–133
    "COPYCAT," 64–65, 67, 79, 87, 126, 169
    dont smile at me, 67–69, 75, 88, 106
    "everything i wanted," 194–195, 203
    "Fingers Crossed," 27, 32
    "hostage," 44, 68, 111–113
    "idontwannabeyouanymore," 65, 91–92
    "ilomilo," 156–157, 165
    "limbo," 74–75, 80

"listen before i go," 154, 157
"lovely," 105–107, 119, 133
"my boy," 44, 57, 66, 68, 89, 99–100,
    126
"New Girl," 94, 177
"Nightmare," 194
"No Time to Die," 7, 208
"ocean eyes," 28, 30–33, 37, 39–41,
    43–44, 49–50, 53, 55, 61–62,
    64, 66, 68, 77, 80, 87–88, 91–92,
    105, 115, 126, 128, 137, 144, 167,
    176–177, 201, 207
"party favor," 44, 68, 75, 87, 94, 113
"sHE's brOKen," 26–27
"Six Feet Under," 41, 43–44, 50
various covers, 73–74, 95, 113, 129,
    144, 205
various titles, 156–157
"watch," 77, 90, 138
"What a Wonderful Life," 13
"WHEN I WAS OLDER," 138–139, 143
"when the party's over," 94, 101,
    129–131, 133, 154, 156, 204
*When We All Fall Asleep, Where Do We
    Go?*, 74, 140, 154, 164, 168, 175,
    183, 188
"wish you were gay," 81, 144, 154, 156
"xanny," 155, 157–159, 202
"you should see me in a crown,"
    116–118, 120, 126, 152, 154–155

Nash, Kate, 54
Nashville, TN, 195
Neighbourhood at the Shrine, 29
Netflix, 54, 139
Netherlands, the, 107, 143, 169
"New Girl" (Finneas), 94, 177
New Music Friday (Spotify), 57
New York, 14, 79, 87, 102, 104, 113, 131,
    179, 188
New York Fashion Week, 119
New York Times, 29, 128, 204
New Zealand, 18, 113, 168, 177
    "bury a friend," 142
    first hits, 89, 125
    growing fan base, 69
    Laneway, 92
    "lovely," 106–107
    sold out shows, 75
    "when the party's over," 131
    "you should see me in a crown," 119

Next Models, 120
Nirvana, 129, 144
NME, 56, 179, 211
"No Music on a Dead Planet" (climate
    change slogan), 196
Norway, 107, 131, 195
No Time to Die, 208
Novak, B. J., 157
Nylon Germany, 169
Nylon magazine, 88
NZ Herald, 76

Oakland, CA, 127
O'Connell, Billie Eilish Pirate Baird.
    See career of Billie Eilish; music of
    Billie Eilish; personal life of Billie
    Eilish; styling of Billie Eilish
O'Connell, Finneas, 8, 28, 33, 53–54, 66,
    75, 87, 106, 140, 175–183
    "bad guy," 154
    Billie's "Pirate" moniker, 14
    early film roles, 16–17, 25
    enduring relationship with Billie, 17, 20,
        39–41, 50–51, 57, 61–62, 69, 127,
        176, 203
    homeschooling, 16–17
    "ocean eyes," 30–31
    piano playing, 44, 64, 77, 94, 130
    Slightlys, the, 25, 30
    ukulele, 15
    uploading to SoundCloud, 26–27, 29
    "when the party's over," 130–131
O'Connell, Patrick, 14–16, 78–79
Office, The, 79, 156–157
"Off to the Races" (Lana Del Rey), 19
Okeechobee Music & Arts Festival, 99
1 by 1 Tour, 121, 126, 131, 142–147, 179
Onfroy, Jahseh. *See* XXXTentacion
Oregon, 79
Osaka, Japan, 119
Oscars, 139, 205, 207, 209
Osheaga, Montreal, Canada, 114
Oslo, Norway, 99
Other Stage, Glastonbury, UK, 170
Outdoor Theatre, Coachella, 165
Outside Lands, San Francisco, CA, 114
OYOY label, 179

Paris, France, 83, 99
Park, Megan, 76
Pawsitive Change Prison Program, 192

Peaches, 181
Peacock, Matty, 112
Pepper, 15
personal life of Billie Eilish
    a teenager, 55–56
    Billie's Closet, 192
    birth, 13
    body image issues, 169–170, 210–211
    character, 7–8
    depression, 80, 91, 170, 189
    eighteenth birthday, 202–203
    enduring relationship with Finneas, 17,
        20, 39–41, 50–51, 57, 61–62, 69,
        127, 176, 203
    environmental concerns, 210
    fame, attitude to, 194–195
    family, 13–15
    favorite singers and music, 19, 114
    feminism, 81–82
    first car, 138
    food preferences, 104
    Highland Park home, 14–15
    homeschooling, 16–17
    horses, love of, 18
    ice skating, 137
    mental health issues, 170, 189
    origins of name, 13–14
    pets, 15
    sleep paralysis, 153
    synesthesia, 158–159
    Tourette's Syndrome, 63
    veganism, 103–104
Phantogram, 144
Philadelphia, PA, 79–80, 113, 169
Pigeons & Planes, 88
Pixar, 132
Planned Parenthood Federation, 82, 193
Platoon, 38, 41, 51, 57
Pollstar, 114
Pop Remix (Spotify), 57
Porter, Billy, 205
Prada, 209
Pretty Little Liars, 41
Princess Nokia, 82
Pryzm Club, 145
"Put Your Head on My Shoulder" (Anka),
    126
Pyramid Stage, Glastonbury, UK, 170

Quinn, Colin, 189

Raine, Mehki, 28, 141
Ramona and Beezus, 17
Randall's Island Park, New York, 107
Recording Industry Association of America (RIAA), 92
Record Store Day, 113
Red Rocks Amphitheatre, CO, 169
"Reichenbach Fall, The" (BBC *Sherlock*), 117
Reverb, 210
Revolution Dance Center (RDC), Los Angeles, CA, 26
Reyez, Jessie, 82, 129
Rickshaw Stop, San Francisco, CA, 44
Roberts, Julia, 197
Robyn, 74
Rockin'On, 169
Rolling Stone magazine, 17, 79, 91, 196
Roma (Cuarón), 138–139
Romance (Cabello), 182
Rosalía, 146
"Royals" (Lorde), 20
Royal Wedding (Donen), 190
Rukasin, Danny, 33
"Runaway" (Aurora), 19

Saint Petersburg, Russia, 188
San Diego, CA, 53
San Francisco, CA, 44, 99, 114, 194
Santa Monica, CA, 32, 132
   Pier Concerts, 25
Saturday Night Live (*SNL*), 190
Scholfield, Henry, 112
Scott, Travis, 28, 163, 166
Seattle, WA, 78–79
"Seize the Awkward" campaign, 170
Shane, Kodie, 82
Share Your Gifts campaign, 132
"Shelter" (Finneas), 180
Sherlock (BBC), 117–118
Shrine Expo Hall, Los Angeles, CA, 29, 187
Siberia Hills, 165, 210
Silver Lake, Los Angeles, CA, 45
Singapore, 92–93
Ski Mask the Slump God, 28
Slightlys, the, 25, 30, 32–33, 176
Smino, 28
Smith, Jaden, 166
Snapchat, 73, 79
Sniffers magazine, 106–107

"Snippet into Billie's Mind, A" (YouTube), 155
Sofar Sounds, 44
Songkick, 38
Soto Sosa, Manuela, 131
SoundCloud, 26–32, 68, 105, 115, 127
   Billie and Lorde, 20
   Billie on, 7, 39
   "bitches broken hearts," 88
   "limbo," 75
   Saul Klein, 38
   "Six Feet Under," 41
Sound of 2018 list (BBC), 89
South Korea, 119, 142
Spain, 180, 188
Sparks Arena, Auckland, New Zealand, 168
Spotify, 137
   "bellyache," 57
   "bury a friend," 142
   Finneas on, 178
   "ocean eyes," 66
   "Six Feet Under," 41
   "you should see me in a crown," 118
Staples, Vince, 54, 90, 106, 166
Starbucks, 20, 30, 104
"Station" (Låpsley), 29
Stockholm, Sweden, 83, 99
Strokes, the, 102, 176
styling of Billie Eilish
   "Bored" video, 62
   Chanel and Gucci, 205
   Coup De Main cover, 89
   designs own clothes, 125–126
   Ellen DeGeneres Show, 120
   green ensemble, 187–188, 193, 204
   Late Late Show, 77
   launches high street range, 210
   New York Fashion Week, 119
   "ocean eyes" video, 40
   Rickshaw Stop, 45
   Singapore, 93–94
   Sofar Sounds promotion, 44
   Tonight Show, 102
   various preferences, 52
   Where's My Mind Tour, 101
   with Khalid, 106–107
Sulewski, Claudia, 178
Sunday Times, 169
Sweden, 107, 131, 143
Sweet Sound Bites blog, 45

Swift, Taylor, 81, 163, 193, 203
Switzerland, 143
SXSW, Austin, TX, 53, 102, 151
Sydney, Australia, 75

"Tamale" (Tyler, the Creator), 42
Teen Vogue, 45
"Telegraph Ave" (Childish Gambino), 129
Tenants of the Trees, Los Angeles, CA, 45
Third Man Records, Nashville, TN, 195
13 Reasons Why, 54, 57
Thompson, Megan, 40
Thutmose, 78–79, 114
Tidal, 41
Tidal magazine, 153
Tigertown, 92
Time Out, 13
Times Square, New York, 188
Tokyo, Japan, 119, 179
Tonight Show Starring Jimmy Fallon, 102, 189
Toronto, Canada, 79–80, 113, 169
Tourette's syndrome, 63
Trader Joe's, 191
Trevor Project, 145
Triple J, 95
Tulsa, OK, 16
Tumblr, 103
Tuning Fork, Auckland, New Zealand, 94
Twitter, 140
    engaging with fans, 73
    Finneas on, 131, 178
    Florence and the Machine tour, 133
    followers, 91
    importance of for Billie, 206
    Khalid follows, 105
    spilling every thought, 56
    Tyler, the Creator, 28, 41–43, 114

Uber Eats, 104
UK (United Kingdom), 53, 169
    "bad guy," 164
    BBC Sound of 2018 list, 89
    Blood Harmony, 180
    "bury a friend," 142
    "everything i wanted," 195
    Glastonbury, 170
    growing fan base, 64, 69
    "lovely," 107
    Maida Vale Studios, 144
    "No Time to Die," 209

"ocean eyes," 137
    Pryzm Club, 145
    "when the party's over," 131
UNICEF, 193
UN (United Nations), 189
Up Next (Apple), 77
"Used to This" (Cabello), 182

Valentine's Day, 99
Van Halen, 55
Vanity Fair, 8, 111, 137, 191, 197
Variety's Hitmakers brunch, 183
Versace, 209
Vevo, 89
Vevo LIFT, 117, 131
Vice magazine, 52
"Visions" (Cheat Codes), 39
Vogue magazine, 138, 169, 209–210

Walking Dead, The, 27, 117
Washington, DC, 79, 120
We Can Survive concert (Hollywood Bowl), 193
We Sail (Baird), 15
Whack, Tierra, 28
Where Do We Go? World Tour, 210
Wheres My Mind Tour, 88–89, 93, 100, 103, 120
Winehouse, Amy, 19
Wolf (Tyler, the Creator), 42
WWD.com, 120

X-Men, 17
XXXTentacion, 28, 127–128

"Yesterday" (the Beatles), 205
"You Don't Get Me High Anymore" (Phantogram), 144
"Young Dumb & Broke" (Khalid), 133
YouTube, 42, 44, 63, 100, 113, 140, 155, 178, 188, 191
    "6.18.18," 127
    Billie on synesthesia, 158
    Billie performs, 49, 87, 91, 95, 202
    Billie sings a Beatles song, 15
    "bury a friend," 142
    fans make videos, 75
    "lovely," 106, 111

Zimmer, Hans, 209